TO HIM WHO SITS ON THE THRONE

Praising God with the Scriptures

Selected, organized, and highlighted by **Mike Thomas**

To Him Who Sits on the Throne:
Praising God with the Scriptures
Copyright © 2009
By Dr. Michael D. (Mike) Thomas
Temple, Texas

This volume is a revision and re-issue of the book,
Thanksgiving and Praise,
first published in 1989 by J. Countryman

All Scriptures from the King James Version

Copy Editor: Carolyn Anderson

Cover design by Kimberley Doucette

ISBN:
10 - 1514264854
13 - 9781514264850

Contents

Preface (6)

1. Preparation in Prayer & Meditation (9)

2. The Bible Tells Us to …(13)

    Be Glad (15)
    Bless the Lord (17)
    Exalt, Magnify the Lord (20)
    Give Glory, Glorify (21)
    Give Thanks (22)
    Praise, Worship (25)
    Rejoice (30)
    Sing Praises (33)

3. Portraits of Worship Before the Throne (37)

4. Praises, Promises, & Prayers for Hard Times (43)

5. I Praise God Because He is My …(49)

    Defense, Fortress, Strong Tower (51)
    God (53)
    Refuge (56)
    Rock (58)
    Salvation (59)
    Strength (61)

6. I Praise God Because He is …(63)

    Almighty, Over All (65)
    Eternal, Everlasting (67)
    The Father (69)
    God (73)
    Good (77)
    Great (79)
    Holy (83)

>
> **Just (86)**
> **King (87)**
> **Lord (90)**
> **Love (96)**
> **Merciful (99)**
> **Mighty (101)**
> **Patient, Longsuffering (103)**
> **Righteous (105)**
> **Unique, None Like Him (107)**
> **Wise (108)**

7. I Praise God for His …(109)

> **Beauty (111)**
> **Faithfulness (113)**
> **Glory (114)**
> **Grace (117)**
> **Lovingkindness (121)**
> **Majesty (124)**
> **Mercy (126)**
> **Name (130)**
> **Power (134)**
> **Righteousness (136)**
> **Word (138)**

8. I Praise God because He …(141)

> **Delivers (143)**
> **Does Wonders (146)**
> **Forgives (148)**
> **Gives (150)**
> **Hears (153)**
> **Judges Righteously (155)**
> **Knows (158)**
> **Leads, Guides, Directs (160)**
> **Loves, Cares (162)**
> **Made Heaven and Earth (165)**
> **Preserves (168)**
> **Reigns (170)**

　　　　Saves, Redeems (172)
　　　　Teaches (175)

9. Divine Names & Titles (177)

10. Worshiping Jesus (185)

11. I Praise Jesus Because He is …(191)

　　　　King (193)
　　　　The Lamb of God (194)
　　　　Light (196)
　　　　Lord (198)
　　　　Our Savior (200)
　　　　The Son of God (202)
　　　　The Son of Man (207)

12. I Praise Jesus Because He …(209)

　　　　Cares, Has Compassion, Loves (211)
　　　　Has Power & Authority (213)
　　　　Heals (216)
　　　　Suffered & Died for My Sins (220)
　　　　Rose from the Grave (223)
　　　　Shall Return (226)

Personal Notes (229)

PREFACE

One day in the mid-'80s, I was driving to work when the Lord asked me three questions: "How many of My promises do you know by memory?" After reciting many with great enthusiasm, I realized that He already knew the answer and that I needed to listen again. Then, the second question, "How many praise scriptures do you know by heart?" I stumbled and faltered, tried to verbalize a few. It was obvious I didn't know them by heart. The third question: "Why is that?" I thought, because promises are for me, and praise is for Him. And I'm all about me.

This experience sent me on a search into the Bible to mark every praise scripture there. I compiled what I found, and the result was published in 1989 by J. Countryman in a book called *Thanksgiving and Praise*.

The present volume is a revision and re-issue of that work. Changes are based in large part on what I have learned in the last twenty years. In more recent times, in periods of desperation, it has pleased the Lord to call me to Himself and to His Word. I am not sure why, considering my poor record. For weeks, months at a time, I sought Him and His promises like a starving man, as "a deer panting for streams of water." In my extreme anxiety, I flew through the Bible, looking for comfort from the Author. But God said, "Slow down and meditate on just a few verses, even a few words."

All the scriptures contained in this collection are familiar, but we must read them anew, prayerfully, and meditate, especially on key phrases and words (I have highlighted at least one in each passage).

Praising God, knowing God, loving God are all one and the same. Naturally, we want to know God better and praise Him in Spirit and in Truth, but we will never accomplish this on our own terms. We come to know Him as He reveals Himself to us through His Word.

So we return to the Bible, these verses, over and over again, because each time, He shows us something different, something fresh, some new facet of His eternal Being and Love, especially if we take extra time to meditate on the Holy and Awesome God, the One Who is Faithful and True, He Who Has All Power, the Infinite God of Infinite Worth.

And **every creature** which is in heaven, and on the earth, and under the earth, and such as are in the sea, and all that are in them, heard I saying, **Blessing, and honour, and glory, and power**, *be* unto him that sitteth upon the throne, and unto the Lamb for ever and ever.
Revelation 5:13

Preparation in Prayer & Meditation

PREPARATION IN PRAYER & MEDITATION

But if from thence thou shalt seek the LORD thy God, thou shalt find him, if thou seek him **with all thy heart and with all thy soul**. *Deuteronomy 4:29*

Seek the LORD and his strength, seek **his face continually**. *I Chronicles 16:11*

And they **entered into a covenant** to seek the LORD God of their fathers with all their heart and with all their soul. *II Chronicles 15:12*

Enter into **his gates with thanksgiving**, *and* into **his courts with praise**: be thankful unto him, *and* bless his name. *Psalm 100:4*

Then **believed they his words**; they sang his praise. *Psalm 106:12*

Sow to yourselves in righteousness, reap in mercy; **break up your fallow ground**: for it is time to seek the LORD, till he come and rain righteousness upon you. *Hosea 10:12*

And the inhabitants of one city shall go to another, saying, **Let us go speedily to pray before the LORD**, and to seek the LORD of hosts: I will go also. *Zechariah 8:21*

That they should seek the Lord, if haply they might feel after him, and find him, **though he be not far from every one of us**. *Acts 17:27*

Wherefore I also, after I heard of your faith in the Lord Jesus, and love unto all the saints, Cease not to give thanks for you, making mention of you in my prayers; That the God of our Lord Jesus Christ, the Father of glory, may **give unto you the spirit of wisdom and revelation in the knowledge of him**: The eyes of your understanding being enlightened; that ye may know what is the hope of his calling, and what the riches of the glory of his inheritance in the saints, And what *is* **the exceeding greatness of his power to us-ward** who believe, according to the working of his mighty power, Which he wrought in Christ, when he raised him from the dead, and set *him* at his own right hand in the heavenly *places*, Far above all principality, and power, and might, and dominion, and every name that is named, not only in this world, but also in that which is to come: And hath put **all *things* under his feet**, and gave him *to be* the head over all *things* to the church, Which is his body, **the fulness of him that filleth all in all**. *Ephesians 1:15-22*

For this cause I bow my knees unto the Father of our Lord Jesus Christ, Of whom the whole family in heaven and earth is named, That he would grant you, according to the riches of his glory, **to be strengthened with might by his Spirit** in the inner man; That Christ may dwell in your hearts by faith; that ye, being rooted and grounded in love, May be able to comprehend with all saints what *is* the breadth, and length, and depth, and height; **And to know the love of Christ**, which passeth knowledge, that ye might be filled with all the fulness of God. Now unto him that is able to do **exceeding abundantly above all that we ask or think**, according to the power that worketh in us, Unto him *be* glory in the church by Christ Jesus throughout all ages, world without end. Amen. *Ephesians 3:14-21*

Having therefore, brethren, **boldness** to enter into the holiest **by the blood of Jesus,** By a new and living way, which he hath consecrated for us, through the veil, that is to say, his flesh. *Hebrews 10:19-20*

Wherefore we are receiving a kingdom which cannot be moved, let us have grace, whereby we may serve God acceptably with **reverence and godly fear**. *Hebrews 12:28*

Draw nigh to God, and he will draw nigh to you. *James 4:8*

If we confess our sins, he is **faithful and just** to forgive us *our* sins, and to cleanse us from **all** unrighteousness. *I John 1:9*

The Bible Tells Us to…

THE BIBLE TELLS US TO...

Be Glad

Let the heavens be glad, and let the earth rejoice: and let *men* say among the nations, **The LORD reigneth**. *1 Chronicles 16:31*

I will be glad and rejoice in thee: **I will sing praise to thy name**, O thou most High. *Psalm 9:2*

I will be glad and rejoice in thy mercy: for **thou hast considered my trouble**; thou hast known my soul in adversities. *Psalm 31:7*

Be glad in the LORD, and rejoice, ye righteous: and **shout for joy**, all *ye that are* upright in heart. *Psalm 32:11*

Let them shout for joy, and be glad, that favour my righteous cause: yea, let them say continually, Let the LORD be magnified, **which hath pleasure in the prosperity of his servant.** *Psalm 35:27*

Let all those that seek thee rejoice and be glad in thee: let such as **love thy salvation** say continually, The LORD be magnified. *Psalm 40:16*

The righteous shall be glad in the LORD, and shall **trust in him**; and all the upright in heart shall glory. *Psalm 64:10*

O let the nations be glad and sing for joy: for **thou shalt judge the people righteously**, and govern the nations upon earth. *Psalm 67:4*

But let the righteous be glad; let them rejoice before God: yea, **let them exceedingly rejoice.** *Psalm 68:3*

Let all those **that seek thee** rejoice and be glad in thee: and let such as love thy salvation say continually, Let God be magnified. *Psalm 70:4*

O satisfy us early with **thy mercy**; that we may rejoice and be glad all our days. *Psalm 90:14*

My **meditation of him shall be sweet**: I will be glad in the LORD. *Psalm 104:34*

This *is* **the day *which* the LORD hath made**; we will rejoice and be glad in it. *Psalm 118:24*

And it shall be said in that day, Lo, this *is* our God; we have waited for him, and **he will save us**: this *is* the LORD; we have waited for him, we will be glad and rejoice in his salvation. *Isaiah 25:9*

Fear not, O land; be glad and rejoice: for **the LORD will do great things**. *Joel 2:21*

Sing, O daughter of Zion; shout, O Israel; be glad and rejoice **with all the heart**, O daughter of Jerusalem. *Zephaniah 3:14*

But rejoice, inasmuch as ye are partakers of Christ's sufferings; that, **when his glory shall be revealed**, ye may be glad also with exceeding joy. *1 Peter 4:13*

Let us be glad and rejoice, and **give honour to him**: for the marriage of the Lamb is come, and his wife hath made herself ready. *Revelation 19:7*

THE BIBLE TELLS US TO…

Bless the Lord

And David said to all the congregation, Now bless the LORD your God. And all the congregation blessed the LORD God of their fathers, and **bowed down their heads, and worshipped the LORD**, and the king. *I Chronicles 29:20*

Stand up and bless the LORD your God for ever and ever: and **blessed be thy glorious name, which is exalted above all blessing and praise**. *Nehemiah 9:5*

Naked came lout of my mother's womb, and naked shall I return thither: **the LORD gave, and the LORD hath taken away**; blessed be the name of the LORD. *Job 1:21*

I will bless the LORD, who **hath given me counsel**. *Psalm 16:7*

The LORD liveth; and blessed be **my rock**; and let the **God of my salvation** be exalted. *Psalm 18:46*

My foot standeth in an even place: in the congregations will I bless the LORD. *Psalm 26:12*

I will bless the LORD **at all times**: his praise shall continually be in my mouth. *Psalm 34:1*

Blessed be the LORD God of Israel **from everlasting, and to everlasting**. Amen, and Amen. *Psalm 41:13*

Thus will I bless thee while I live: **I will lift up my hands** in thy name. *Psalm 63:4*

O bless our God, ye people, and **make the voice of his praise to be heard**. *Psalm 66:8*

Blessed be God, which **hath not turned away my prayer**, nor his mercy from me. *Psalm 66:20*

Blessed be the Lord, **who daily loadeth us with benefits**, even the God of our salvation. *Psalm 68:19*

Bless ye God in the congregations, even the Lord, from **the fountain of Israel**. *Psalm 68:26*

Blessed be the LORD God, the God of Israel, **who only doeth wondrous things**. And blessed be **his glorious name** for ever: and let the whole earth be filled with his glory; Amen, and Amen. *Psalm 72:18-19*

Sing unto the LORD, bless his name; shew forth his salvation from day to day. *Psalm 96:2*

Bless the LORD, O my soul: and **all that is within me**, bless his holy name. Bless the LORD, O my soul, and **forget not all his benefits**. *Psalm 103:1-2*

Bless the LORD, ye his angels, that excel in strength, that do his commandments, hearkening unto the voice of his word. Bless ye the LORD, all ye his hosts; ye ministers of his, that do his pleasure. Bless the LORD, **all his works in all places of his dominion**: bless the LORD, O my soul. *Psalm 103:20-22*

Bless the LORD, O my soul. O LORD my God, thou art very great; thou art **clothed with honour and majesty**. Who **coverest thyself with light** as with a garment: who stretchest out the heaven like a curtain: Who layeth the beams of his chambers in the waters: who maketh the clouds his chariot: who **walketh upon the wings of the wind**: Who maketh his angels spirits; his ministers a flaming fire. *Psalm 104:1-4*

Blessed be the LORD God of Israel **from everlasting to everlasting**: and let all the people say, Amen. Praise ye the LORD. *Psalm 106:48*

Blessed be the name of the LORD **from this time forth and for evermore**. *Psalm 113:2*

Blessed art thou, O LORD: **teach me thy statutes**. *Psalm 119:12*

Behold, bless ye the LORD, all ye servants of the LORD, which by night stand in the house of the LORD. **Lift up your hands in the sanctuary**, and bless the LORD. The LORD that **made heaven and earth** bless thee out of Zion. *Psalm 134:1-3*

I will extol thee, my God, O king; and I will bless thy name for ever and ever. **Every day** will I bless thee; and I will praise thy name for ever and ever. *Psalm 145:1-2*

All thy works shall praise thee, O LORD; and thy saints shall bless thee. *Psalm 145:10*

My mouth shall speak the praise of the LORD: and let all flesh bless his holy name for ever and ever. *Psalm 145:21*

Blessed be the name of God for ever and ever: for **wisdom and might are his**. *Daniel 2:20*

Blessed be the God and Father of our Lord Jesus Christ, who hath blessed us **with all spiritual blessings in heavenly places** in Christ. *Ephesians 1:3*

Blessed be the God and Father of our Lord Jesus Christ, which according to **his abundant mercy** hath begotten us again unto **a lively hope by the resurrection of Jesus** Christ from the dead. *I Peter 1:3*

THE BIBLE TELLS US TO...

Exalt, Magnify the Lord

The LORD *is* **my strength and song**, and he is become my salvation: he *is* **my God**, and I will prepare him an habitation; my father's God, and I will exalt him. *Exodus 15:2*

Remember that thou magnify **his work**, which men behold. *Job 36:24*

O magnify the LORD with me, and **let us exalt his name together**. *Psalm 34:3*

I will praise the name of God **with a song**, and will magnify him **with thanksgiving**. *Psalm 69:30*

Exalt ye the LORD our God, and **worship at his footstool**; *for* he *is* holy. *Psalm 99:5*

Exalt the LORD our God, and **worship at his holy hill**; for the LORD our God *is* holy. *Psalm 99:9*

Let them exalt him also in the congregation of the people, and **praise him in the assembly of the elders**. *Psalm 107:32*

Thou *art* my God, and I will praise thee: *thou art* **my God,** I will exalt thee. *Psalm 118:28*

O LORD, thou *art* my God; I will exalt thee, I will praise thy name; for **thou hast done wonderful *things*;** *thy* counsels of old *are* faithfulness *and* truth. *Isaiah 25:1*

And Mary said, **My soul** doth magnify the Lord. *Luke 1:46*

THE BIBLE TELLS US TO...

Give Glory, Glorify

My son, give, I pray thee, glory to the LORD God of Israel, and **make confession unto him**. *Joshua 7:19*

Give unto the LORD the **glory due unto his name: bring an offering**, and come before him: worship the LORD in **the beauty of holiness**. *I Chronicles 16:28-29*

I will praise thee, O LORD my God, **with all my heart**: and I will glorify thy name **for evermore**. *Psalm 86:12*

Give unto the LORD, O ye kindreds of the people, give unto the LORD **glory and strength**. *Psalm 96:8*

Not unto us, O LORD, not unto us, but unto thy name give glory, **for thy mercy,** *and* for **thy truth's sake**. *Psalm 115:1*

Let them give glory unto the LORD, and **declare his praise** in the islands. *Isaiah 42:12*

Now the God of patience and consolation grant you to be likeminded one toward another according to Christ Jesus: That ye may **with one mind and one mouth** glorify God, even the Father of our Lord Jesus Christ. *Romans 15:5-6*

But he that glorieth, let him **glory in the Lord**. *II Corinthians 10:17*

Fear God, and give glory to him; for the hour of his judgment is come: and worship **him that made heaven, and earth, and the sea, and the fountains of waters**. *Revelation 14:7*

Who shall not **fear thee**, O Lord, and glorify thy name? for **thou only art holy**: for all nations shall come and worship before thee; for thy judgments are made manifest. *Revelation 15:4*

THE BIBLE TELLS US TO...

Give Thanks

Therefore I will give thanks unto thee, O LORD, among the heathen, and **I will sing praises unto thy name.** *II Samuel 22:50*

Give thanks unto the LORD, **call upon his name**, make known his deeds among the people. *I Chronicles 16:8*

To the end that *my* glory may sing praise to thee, and **not be silent**. O LORD my God, I will give thanks unto thee for ever. *Psalm 30:12*

I will give thee thanks **in the great congregation**: I will praise thee among much people. *Psalm 35:18*

That I may publish with the voice of thanksgiving, and **tell of all thy wondrous works**. *Psalm 26:7*

I will praise the name of God with a song, **and will magnify him** with thanksgiving. *Psalm 69:30*

Unto thee, O God, do we give thanks, *unto thee* do we give thanks: for *that* **thy name is near** thy wondrous works declare. *Psalm 75:1*

So **we thy people and sheep of thy pasture** will give thee thanks for ever: we will show forth thy praise to all generations. *Psalm 79:13*

It is a good thing to give thanks unto the LORD, and to sing praises unto thy name, O most High. *Psalm 92:1*

Let us come before his presence with thanksgiving, and make **a joyful noise** unto him with psalms. *Psalm 95:2*

Rejoice in the LORD, ye righteous; and give thanks **at the remembrance of his holiness**. *Psalm 97:12*

Enter into his gates with thanksgiving, and **into his courts** with praise: be thankful unto him, and bless his name. *Psalm 100:4*

O give thanks unto the LORD; call upon his name: **make known his deeds** among the people. *Psalm 105:1*

Save us, O LORD our God, and gather us from among the heathen, to give thanks unto **thy holy name**, *and* to triumph in thy praise. *Psalm 106:47*

I will offer to thee the **sacrifice of thanksgiving**, and will call upon the name of the LORD. *Psalm 116:17*

At midnight I will rise to give thanks unto thee **because of thy righteous judgments**. *Psalm 119:62*

O give thanks unto the God of gods: **for his mercy endureth for ever**. o give thanks to the Lord of lords: for his mercy endureth for ever. *Psalm 136:2-3*

Sing unto the LORD with thanksgiving; sing praise upon the harp unto our God. *Psalm 147:7*

But I will sacrifice unto thee with the voice of thanksgiving; I will pay *that* that I have vowed. Salvation *is* of the LORD. *Jonah 2:9*

But thanks be to God, which **giveth us the victory** through our Lord Jesus Christ. *I Corinthians 15:57*

Now thanks be unto God, which always **causeth us to triumph** in Christ, and maketh manifest the savour of his knowledge by us in every place. *II Corinthians 2:14*

Thanks be unto God for **his unspeakable gift**. *II Corinthians 9:15*

Giving thanks **always for all things** unto God and the Father in the name of our Lord Jesus Christ. *Ephesians 5:20*

Be careful for nothing; but **in every thing by prayer and supplication** with thanksgiving let your requests be made known unto God. *Philippians 4:6*

Giving thanks unto the Father, which hath made us meet to be partakers of **the inheritance of the saints in light**. *Colossians 1:12*

As ye have therefore received Christ Jesus the Lord, so walk ye in him: Rooted and built up in him, and stablished in the faith, as ye have been taught, **abounding** therein with thanksgiving. *Colossians 2:6-7*

And let the **peace of God rule in your hearts**, to the which also ye are called in one body; and be ye thankful. *Colossians 3:15*

Continue in prayer, and watch in the same with thanksgiving. *Colossians 4:2*

In every thing give thanks: for this is **the will of God** in Christ Jesus concerning you. *1 Thessalonians 5:18*

By him therefore let us offer the sacrifice of praise to God continually, that is, **the fruit of our lips** giving thanks to his name. *Hebrews 13:15*

Saying, Amen: Blessing, and glory, and wisdom, and thanksgiving, and honour, and power, and might, *be* unto our God **for ever and ever**. Amen. *Revelation 7:12*

Saying, We give thee thanks, O Lord God Almighty, which art, and wast, and art to come; because thou hast taken to thee **thy great power**, and hast reigned. *Revelation 11:17*

THE BIBLE TELLS US TO...

Praise, Worship

I will bless the LORD at all times: his praise shall **continually be in my mouth**. *Psalm 4:1*

Rejoice in the LORD, O ye righteous: *for* praise is **comely for the upright**. *Psalm 33:1*

And my tongue shall speak of thy righteousness and of thy praise **all the day long**. *Psalm 35:28*

And he hath put **a new song in my mouth**, *even* praise unto our God: many shall see *it*, and fear, and shall trust in the LORD. *Psalm 40:3*

Why art thou cast down, O my soul? and why art thou disquieted within me? hope in God: for **I shall yet praise him**, who is the health of my countenance, and my God. *Psalm 43:5*

In God we boast all the day long, and praise thy name for ever. *Psalm 44:8*

According to thy name, O God, so is thy praise **unto the ends of the earth**: thy right hand is full of righteousness. *Psalm 48:10*

O Lord, **open thou my lips**; and my mouth shall shew forth thy praise. *Psalm 51:15*

I will praise thee for ever, **because thou hast done it**: and I will wait on thy name; for it is good before thy saints. *Psalm 52:9*

In God will I praise *his* **word**: in the LORD will I praise *his* word. *Psalm 56:10*

Because **thy lovingkindness is better than life**, my lips shall praise thee. *Psalm 63:3*

Let the people praise thee, O God; let **all the people** praise thee. *Psalm 67:3*

I will praise the name of God **with a song**, and will magnify him with thanksgiving. *Psalm 69:30*

Let my mouth be filled with thy praise and **with thy honour** all the day. *Psalm 71:8*

But **I will hope continually**, and will yet praise thee **more and more**. *Psalm 71:14*

I will praise thee, O Lord my God, **with all my heart**: and I will glorify thy name for evermore. *Psalm 86:12*

And the heavens shall praise **thy wonders**, O LORD: **thy faithfulness** also in the congregation of the saints. *Psalm 89:5*

O come, let us worship and **bow down**: let us **kneel** before the LORD our maker. *Psalm 95:6*

O worship the LORD in the **beauty of holiness**: fear before him, all the earth. *Psalm 96:9*

Let them praise **thy great and terrible name**; for it is holy. Exalt ye the LORD our God, and worship at his footstool; for he is holy. *Psalm 99:3, 5*

Enter into his gates **with thanksgiving**, and into his courts with praise: be thankful unto him, and **bless his name**. *Psalm 100:4*

Praise ye the LORD. O give thanks unto the LORD; for he is good: for his mercy endureth for ever. Who can utter the mighty acts of the LORD? **who can shew forth all his praise?** *Psalm 106:1-2*

They **believed his words**; they sang his praise. *Psalm 106:12*

O that *men* would praise the LORD *for* **his goodness**, and *for* his wonderful works to the children of men! *Psalm 107:21*

Praise ye the LORD. I will praise the LORD with *my* whole heart, **in the assembly of the upright**, and *in* the congregation. *Psalm 111:1*

Open to me the gates of righteousness: I will go into them, and I will praise the LORD. I will praise thee: for thou hast heard me, and art become **my salvation**. *Psalm 118:19, 21*

Thou *art* my God, and I will praise thee: *thou art* my God, I will exalt thee. *Psalm 118:28*

Seven times a day do I praise thee because of **thy righteous judgments**. *Psalm 119:164*

My lips shall utter praise, when **thou hast taught me thy statutes**. *Psalm 119:171*

Praise ye the LORD. Praise ye **the name of the LORD**; praise *him*, O ye servants of the LORD. *Psalm 135:1*

I will worship toward thy holy temple, and praise thy name for thy lovingkindness and for thy truth: for **thou hast magnified thy word** above all thy name. *Psalm 138:2*

I will praise thee; for I am fearfully and wonderfully made: **marvellous are thy works**; and that my soul knoweth right well. *Psalm 139:14*

Bring my soul out of prison, that I may praise thy name: the righteous shall compass me about; for thou shalt deal **bountifully** with me. *Psalm 142:7*

Every day will I bless thee; and I will praise thy name for ever and ever. One generation shall praise thy works to another, and shall **declare thy mighty acts**. All thy works shall praise thee, O LORD; and thy saints shall bless thee. My mouth shall speak the praise of the LORD: and let all flesh bless his holy name for ever and ever. *Psalm 145:2, 4, 10, 21*

Praise ye the LORD. Praise the LORD, **O my soul**. *Psalm 146:1*

Praise ye him, **all his angels**: praise ye him, all his hosts. *Psalm 148:2*

Let them praise the name of the LORD: for **he commanded, and they were created**. *Psalm 148:5*

Let them praise the name of the LORD: for **his name alone is excellent**;

his glory *is* above the earth and heaven. *Psalm 148:13*

Praise ye the LORD. Praise God in his sanctuary: praise him in the firmament of his power. Praise him for his mighty acts: praise him according to **his excellent greatness. Let every thing that hath breath** praise the LORD. Praise ye the LORD. *Psalm 150:1-2, 6*

Praise the LORD, **call upon his name**, declare his doings among the people, make mention that his name is exalted. *Isaiah 12:4*

O LORD, thou *art* my God; I will exalt thee, I will praise thy name; for thou hast done wonderful *things; thy* **counsels of old** *are* **faithfulness** *and* **truth.** *Isaiah 25:1*

This people have I formed for myself; they shall **show forth my praise.** *Isaiah 43:21*

For as the earth bringeth forth her bud, and as the garden causeth the things that are sown in it to spring forth; so the Lord GOD will **cause righteousness and praise to spring forth before all the nations.** *Isaiah 61:11*

Heal me, O LORD, and **I shall be healed**; save me, and **I shall be saved**: for thou art my praise. *Jeremiah 17:14*

And ye shall eat in plenty, and be satisfied, and praise the name of the LORD your God, that hath **dealt wondrously with you**: and my people shall never be ashamed. *Joel 2:26*

God came from Teman, and the Holy One from mount Paran. *Selah.* **His glory covered the heavens**, and the earth was full of his praise. *Habakkuk 3:3*

And when he was come nigh, even now at the descent of the mount of Olives, the whole multitude of the disciples began to **rejoice and praise God with a loud voice** for all the mighty works that they had seen. *Luke 19:37*

By him therefore let us offer **the sacrifice of praise** to God continually, that is, the fruit of our lips giving thanks to his name. *Hebrews 13:15*

But ye are a chosen generation, a royal priesthood, an holy nation, a peculiar people; that ye should shew forth the praises of him who hath **called you out of darkness into his marvellous light**. *I Peter 2:9*

And a voice came out of the throne, saying, Praise our God, all ye his servants, and ye that fear him, **both small and great**. *Revelation 19:5*

THE BIBLE TELLS US TO...

Rejoice

Rejoice, **O ye nations**, with his people. *Deuteronomy 32:43*

Glory ye in his holy name: let the heart of them rejoice that seek the LORD. *1 Chronicles 16:10*

Let the heavens be glad, and let the earth rejoice: and let *men* say among the nations, **The LORD reigneth**. *1 Chronicles 16:31*

Serve the LORD with fear, and rejoice **with trembling**. *Psalm 2:11*

But let all those that **put their trust in thee** rejoice: let them ever shout for joy, because **thou defendest them**: let them also that love thy name be joyful in thee. *Psalm 5:11*

We will rejoice in thy salvation, and **in the name of our God** we will set up our banners: the LORD fulfill all thy petitions. *Psalm 20:5*

I will be glad and rejoice in thy mercy: for **thou hast considered my trouble; thou hast known my soul in adversities**. *Psalm 31:7*

Be glad in the LORD, and rejoice, ye righteous: and **shout for joy**, all ye that are upright in heart. *Psalm 32:11*

Rejoice in the LORD, O ye righteous: for **praise is comely for the upright**. *Psalm 33:1*

For our heart shall rejoice in him, because **we have trusted in his holy name**. *Psalm 33:21*

And **my soul** shall be joyful in the LORD: it shall rejoice in his salvation. *Psalm 35:9*

Let all those that **seek thee** rejoice and be glad in thee: let such as love thy salvation say continually, The LORD be magnified. *Psalm 40:16*

Because **thou hast been my help**, therefore in the shadow of thy wings will I rejoice. *Psalm 63:7*

But let the righteous be glad; let them rejoice before God: yea, let them **exceedingly** rejoice. Sing unto God, sing praises to his name: extol him that rideth upon the heavens by his name JAH, and rejoice before him. *Psalm 68:3-4*

Let all those that seek thee rejoice and be glad in thee: and let such as **love thy salvation** say continually, Let God be magnified. *Psalm 70:4*

My lips shall greatly rejoice when I sing unto thee; and **my soul, which thou hast redeemed**. *Psalm 71:23*

Wilt thou not **revive us again**: that thy people may rejoice in thee? *Psalm 85:6*

In thy name shall they rejoice **all the day**: and in thy righteousness shall they be exalted. *Psalm 89:16*

O satisfy us early with **thy mercy**; that we may rejoice and be glad all our days. *Psalm 90:14*

Rejoice in the LORD, ye righteous; and give thanks **at the remembrance of his holiness**. *Psalm 97:12*

Make a joyful noise unto the LORD all the earth: make a loud noise, and rejoice, and sing praise. *Psalm 98:4*

Glory ye in **his holy name**: let the heart of them rejoice that seek the LORD. *Psalm 105:3*

This is **the day which the LORD hath made**; we will rejoice and be glad in it. *Psalm 118:24*

I rejoice at thy word, as one that findeth **great spoil**. *Psalm 119:162*

I will greatly rejoice in the LORD, my soul shall be joyful in my God; for he hath clothed me with the **garments of salvation**, he hath covered me with the **robe of righteousness**, as a bridegroom decketh himself with ornaments, and as a bride adorneth herself with her jewels. *Isaiah 61:10*

Fear not, O land; be glad and rejoice: for the LORD **will do great things**. *Joel 2:21*

Yet I will rejoice in the LORD, I will joy in the **God of my salvation**. *Habakkuk 3:18*

Rejoice **greatly**, O daughter of Zion; shout, O daughter of Jerusalem: behold, thy King cometh unto thee: he *is* just, and having salvation; lowly, and riding upon an ass, and upon a colt the foal of an ass. *Zechariah 9:9*

Rejoice, and be exceeding glad: for **great *is* your reward in heaven**: for so persecuted they the prophets which were before you. *Matthew 5:12*

Notwithstanding in this rejoice not, that the spirits are subject unto you; but rather rejoice, **because your names are written in heaven**. *Luke 10:20*

By whom also we have access by faith into this grace wherein we stand, and rejoice in **hope of the glory of God**. *Romans 5:2*

Rejoice **with them that do rejoice**, and weep with them that weep. *Romans 12:15*

Rejoice in the Lord **alway**: *and* again I say, Rejoice. *Philippians 4:4*

Rejoice **evermore**. *I Thessalonians 5:16*

Whom having not seen, ye love; in whom, though now ye see him not, yet believing, ye rejoice with joy **unspeakable and full of glory**. *I Peter 1:8*

But rejoice, inasmuch as ye are partakers of Christ's sufferings; that, **when his glory shall be revealed**, ye may be glad also with exceeding joy. *1 Peter 4:13*

Let us be glad and rejoice, and **give honour to him**: for the marriage of the Lamb is come, and his wife hath made herself ready. *Revelation 19:7*

THE BIBLE TELLS US TO...

Sing Praises

Hear, O ye kings; give ear, O ye princes; I, *even* I, will sing unto the LORD; I will sing *praise* **to the LORD God of Israel**. *Judges 5:3*

Therefore I will **give thanks unto thee**, O LORD, among the heathen, and I will sing praises unto thy name. *II Samuel 22:50*

Sing unto him, **sing psalms unto him**, talk ye of all his wondrous works. *I Chronicles 16:9*

Sing unto the LORD, all the earth; **shew forth from day to day his salvation**. *I Chronicles 16:23*

And when they began to sing and to praise, the LORD set ambushments against the children of Ammon, Moab, and mount Seir, which were come against Judah; and **they were smitten**. *II Chronicles 20:22*

Moreover Hezekiah the king and the princes commanded the Levites to sing praise unto the LORD with the words of David, and of Asaph the seer. And they sang praises with gladness, and **they bowed their heads and worshipped**. *II Chronicles 29:30*

I will praise the LORD **according to his righteousness**: and will sing praise to the name of the LORD most high. *Psalm 7:17*

Sing praises to the LORD, which dwelleth in Zion: **declare among the people his doings**. *Psalm 9:11*

I will sing unto the LORD, because **he hath dealt bountifully with me**. *Psalm 13:6*

Be thou exalted, LORD, in thine own strength: so will we sing and praise **thy power**. *Psalm 21:13*

To the end that *my* glory may sing praise to thee, and **not be silent**. O LORD my God, I will give thanks unto thee for ever. *Psalm 30:12*

Praise the LORD with **harp**: sing unto him with the **psaltery** *and* an

instrument of ten strings. *Psalm 33:2*

And he hath **put a new song in my mouth**, even praise unto our God: many shall see it, and fear, and shall trust in the LORD. *Psalm 40:3*

Sing praises to God, sing praises: sing praises unto our King, sing praises. For God is the King of all the earth: sing ye praises **with understanding**. *Psalm 47:6-7*

So will I sing praise unto thy name for ever, that I may **daily perform my vows**. *Psalm 61:8*

Sing forth the honour of his name: **make his praise glorious**. All the earth shall worship thee, and shall sing unto thee; they shall sing unto thy name. *Psalm 66:2, 4*

Let the nations be glad and sing for joy: for **thou shalt judge the people righteously**, and govern the nations upon earth. *Psalms 67:4*

Sing unto God, sing praises to his name: **extol him that rideth upon the heavens** by his name JAH, and rejoice before him. *Psalm 68:4*

I will also praise thee with the psaltery, *even* thy truth, O my God: unto thee will I sing with the harp, **O thou Holy One of Israel**. *Psalm 71:22*

But I will declare for ever; I will sing praises to the God of Jacob. *Psalm 75:9*

I will sing of the **mercies of the LORD for ever**: with my mouth will I make known thy faithfulness to all generations. *Psalm 89:1*

It is a good thing to give thanks unto the LORD, and to sing praises unto thy name, O most High: To shew forth **thy lovingkindness** in the morning, and **thy faithfulness** every night, Upon an instrument often strings, and upon the psaltery; upon the harp with a solemn sound. *Psalm 92:1-3*

Come, let us sing unto the LORD: let us make a joyful noise to **the rock of our salvation**. *Psalm 95:1*

Sing unto the LORD a new song: sing unto the LORD, all the earth. Sing unto the LORD, **bless his name**; shew forth his salvation from day to day. *Psalm 96:1, 2*

Sing unto the LORD a new song; for he hath done marvellous things: **his right hand, and his holy arm, hath gotten him the victory**. Make a joyful noise unto the LORD, all the earth: make a loud noise, and rejoice, and sing praise. Sing unto the LORD with the harp; with the harp, and the voice of a psalm. With trumpets and sound of cornet make a joyful noise before the LORD, the King. *Psalm 98:1, 4-6*

Serve the LORD with gladness: come before his presence with singing. *Psalm 100:2*

O God, **my heart is fixed**; I will sing and give praise, even with my glory. *Psalm 108:1*

Praise the LORD; for the LORD is good: sing praises unto his name; for **it is pleasant**. *Psalm 135:3*

I will praise thee **with my whole heart**: before the gods will I sing praise unto thee. *Psalm 138:1*

While I live will I praise the LORD: I will sing praises unto my God while I have any being. *Psalm 146:2*

Praise ye the LORD: for **it is good to sing praises unto our God**; for it is pleasant; and praise is comely. Sing unto the LORD with thanksgiving; sing praise upon the harp unto our God. *Psalm 147:1, 7*

Praise ye the LORD. Sing unto the LORD a new song, and his praise in the congregation of saints. **Let them praise his name in the dance**: let them sing praises unto him with the timbrel and harp. **Let them sing aloud on their beds**. *Psalm 149:1, 3, 5*

Sing unto the LORD; for **he hath done excellent things**: this is known in all the earth. *Isaiah 12:5*

Sing, O ye heavens; for **the LORD hath done it**: shout, ye lower parts of the earth: break forth in singing, ye mountains, O forest, and every tree therein: for the LORD hath redeemed Jacob, and glorified himself in Israel. *Isaiah 44:23*

Sing, O heavens; and be joyful, O earth; and break forth into singing, O mountains: for the LORD **hath comforted his people**, and will have mercy upon his afflicted. *Isaiah 49:13*

Sing unto the LORD, praise ye the LORD: for **he hath delivered** the soul of the poor from the hand of evildoers. *Jeremiah 20:13*

Sing, O daughter of Zion; shout, O Israel; be glad and **rejoice with all the heart**, O daughter of Jerusalem. *Zephaniah 3:14*

And at midnight Paul and Silas prayed, and sang praises unto God: and the prisoners heard them. And suddenly there was a great earthquake, so that the foundations of the prison were shaken: and **immediately all the doors were opened, and every one's bands were loosed.** *Acts 16:25-26*

Speaking to yourselves in psalms and hymns and spiritual songs, singing and **making melody in your heart to the Lord.** *Ephesians 5:19*

Let the word of Christ dwell in you richly in all wisdom; teaching and admonishing one another in psalms and hymns and spiritual songs, **singing with grace in your hearts** to the Lord. *Colossians 3:16*

Is any among you afflicted? let him pray. **Is any merry?** let him sing psalms. *James 5:13*

Saying, I will declare thy name unto my brethren, **in the midst of the church** will I sing praise unto thee. *Hebrews 2:12*

Portraits of Worship Before the Throne

PORTRAITS OF WORSHIP BEFORE THE THRONE

Isaiah 6:1-8
In the year that king Uzziah died I saw also the Lord sitting upon a throne, **high and lifted up**, and **his train filled the temple**. Above it stood the seraphims: each one had six wings; with twain he covered his face, and with twain he covered his feet, and with twain he did fly. And one cried unto another, and said, **Holy, holy, holy**, *is* the LORD of hosts: **the whole earth** *is* **full of his glory**. And the posts of the door moved at the voice of him that cried, and the house was filled with smoke.

Then said I, Woe *is* me! for I am undone; because I *am* a man of unclean lips, and I dwell in the midst of a people of unclean lips: for mine eyes have seen the King, the LORD of hosts. Then flew one of the seraphims unto me, having a live coal in his hand, *which* he had taken with the tongs from off the altar: And he laid *it* upon my mouth, and said, Lo, this hath touched thy lips; and thine iniquity is taken away, and **thy sin purged**. Also I heard the voice of the Lord, saying, Whom shall I send, and who will go for us? Then said I, **Here** *am* **I; send me**.

Ezekiel 1:26-28
And above the firmament that *was* over their heads *was* the likeness of a throne, as the **appearance of a sapphire stone**: and upon the likeness of the throne *was* the likeness as the appearance of a man above upon it. And I saw as the colour of amber, as the **appearance of fire** round about within it, from the appearance of his loins even upward, and from the appearance of his loins even downward, I saw as it were the appearance of fire, and it had brightness round about. As **the appearance of the bow that is in the cloud** in the day of rain, so *was* the appearance of the brightness round about. This *was* the appearance of the likeness of the **glory of the LORD**. And when I saw *it*, I fell upon my face, and I heard a voice of one that spake.

Daniel 7:9-10
I beheld till the thrones were cast down, and the Ancient of days did sit, **whose garment** *was* **white as snow, and the hair of his head like the pure wool**: **his throne** *was like* **the fiery flame,** *and* **his wheels** *as* **burning fire. A fiery stream issued and came forth from before him**: thousand thousands ministered unto him, and ten thousand times ten thousand stood before him: the judgment was set, and the books were opened.

Revelation 4:1-11

After this I looked, and, behold, a door *was* opened in heaven: and the first voice which I heard *was* as it were of a trumpet talking with me; which said, Come up hither, and I will show thee things which must be hereafter. And immediately I was in the spirit: and, behold, a throne was set in heaven, and *one* sat on the throne. **And he that sat was to look upon like a jasper and a sardine stone**: and *there was* **a rainbow round about the throne, in sight like unto an emerald**. And round about the throne *were* four and twenty seats: and upon the seats I saw four and twenty elders sitting, clothed in white raiment; and they had on their heads crowns of gold. And out of the throne proceeded **lightnings and thunderings** and voices: and *there were* **seven lamps of fire** burning before the throne, which are the seven Spirits of God. And before the throne *there was* **a sea of glass like unto crystal**: and in the midst of the throne, and round about the throne, *were* four beasts full of eyes before and behind. And the first beast *was* like a lion, and the second beast like a calf, and the third beast had a face as a man, and the fourth beast *was* like a flying eagle.

Worship by the twenty-four elders and four living creatures:

And the four beasts had each of them six wings about *him*; and *they were* full of eyes within: and they rest not day and night, saying, **Holy, holy, holy, Lord God Almighty, which was, and is, and is to come.** And when those beasts give glory and honour and thanks to him that sat on the throne, who liveth for ever and ever, The four and twenty elders **fall down before him that sat on the throne, and worship him that liveth for ever and ever, and cast their crowns before the throne**, saying, Thou art worthy, O Lord, to receive **glory and honour and power: for thou hast created all things**, and for thy pleasure they are and were created.

Revelation 5:6-14
Worship from 100,000,000 angels:

And I beheld, and, lo, in the midst of the throne and of the four beasts, and in the midst of the elders, stood a Lamb as it had been slain, having seven horns and seven eyes, which are the seven Spirits of God sent forth

into all the earth. And he came and took the book out of the right hand of him that sat upon the throne. And when he had taken the book, the four beasts and four *and* twenty elders **fell down before the Lamb**, having every one of them harps, and golden vials full of odours, which are the prayers of saints.
And they sung a new song, saying, **Thou art worthy to take the book, and to open the seals thereof: for thou wast slain, and hast redeemed us to God by thy blood** out of every kindred, and tongue, and people, and nation; And hast made us unto our God kings and priests: and we shall reign on the earth. And I beheld, and I heard **the voice of many angels** round about the throne and the beasts and the elders: and the number of them was ten thousand times ten thousand, and thousands of thousands; Saying with a loud voice, **Worthy is the Lamb that was slain to receive power, and riches, and wisdom, and strength, and honour, and glory, and blessing.**

Worship from every creature in heaven, on earth, and under the earth:

And **every creature** which is in heaven, and on the earth, and under the earth, and such as are in the sea, and all that are in them, heard I saying, **Blessing, and honour, and glory, and power,** *be* unto him that sitteth upon the throne, and unto the Lamb for ever and ever. And the four beasts said, Amen. And **the four *and* twenty elders fell down and worshipped him that liveth for ever and ever**.

Revelation 7:9-12
Worship from the vast multitude:

After this I beheld, and, lo, a great multitude, which no man could number, of all nations, and kindreds, and people, and tongues, stood before the throne, and before the Lamb, clothed with white robes, and palms in their hands; And cried with a loud voice, saying, **Salvation to our God which sitteth upon the throne, and unto the Lamb.** And all the angels stood round about the throne, and *about* the elders and the four beasts, and fell before the throne on their faces, and worshipped God, Saying, Amen: **Blessing, and glory, and wisdom, and thanksgiving, and honour, and power, and might,** *be* unto our God for ever and ever. Amen.

Praises, Promises, & Prayers
In Hard Times

PRAISE, PROMISES, & PRAYERS IN HARD TIMES

Is **any thing too hard** for the LORD? *Genesis 18:14*

Shall not **the Judge** of all the earth **do right**? *Genesis 18:25*

For the eyes of the LORD run to and fro throughout the whole earth, to show himself **strong** in the behalf of *them* whose heart *is* perfect toward him. *II Chronicles 16:9*

For I know *that* **my redeemer liveth**, and *that* he shall stand at the latter *day* upon the earth. *Job 19:25*

I had fainted, unless I had believed to see the goodness of the LORD in the land of the living. **Wait on the LORD: be of good courage**, and he shall strengthen thine heart: wait, I say, on the LORD. *Psalm 27:13-14*

Why art thou cast down, O my soul? and why art thou disquieted within me? hope thou in God: for **I shall yet praise him**, *who is* the health of my countenance, and my God. *Psalm 42:11*

God *is* **our refuge and strength**, a very present help in trouble.
Therefore will not we fear, though the earth be removed, and though the mountains be carried into the midst of the sea;
Though the waters thereof roar *and* be troubled, *though* the mountains shake with the swelling thereof. *Psalm 46:1-3.*

Trust in the LORD with **all thine heart**; and **lean not unto thine own understanding**. In all thy ways acknowledge him, and he shall direct thy paths. *Proverbs 3:5-6*

But they that wait upon the LORD **shall renew *their* strength**; they shall mount up **with wings as eagles**; they shall run, and not be weary; *and* they shall walk, and not faint. *Isaiah 40:31*

Fear thou not; for I *am* with thee: be not dismayed; for I *am* thy God: I will strengthen thee; yea, I will help thee; yea, **I will uphold thee** with the right hand of my righteousness. *Isaiah 41:10*

But now thus saith the LORD that created thee, O Jacob, and he that formed thee, O Israel, Fear not: for I have redeemed thee, I have called *thee* by thy name; thou *art* mine. When thou passest through the waters, I *will be* with thee; and through the rivers, **they shall not overflow thee**: when thou walkest through the fire, **thou shalt not be burned**; neither shall the flame kindle upon thee. *Isaiah 43:1-2*

This I recall to my mind, therefore have I hope. *It is of* the LORD'S mercies that we are not consumed, because **his compassions fail not**. *They are* new every morning: great *is* thy faithfulness. The LORD *is* my portion, saith my soul; therefore will I hope in him. The LORD *is* **good unto them that wait for him**, to the soul *that* **seeketh him**. *It is* good that *a man* should both hope and quietly wait for the salvation of the LORD. *Lamentations 3:21-26*

Come unto me, all *ye* that labour and are heavy laden, and **I will give you rest**. Take my yoke upon you, and learn of me; for I am meek and lowly in heart: and ye shall find rest unto your souls. ³⁰For my yoke *is* easy, and my burden is light. *Matthew 11:28-29*

Likewise the Spirit also helpeth our infirmities: for we know not what we should pray for as we ought: but the Spirit itself maketh intercession for us with groanings which cannot be uttered. And he that searcheth the hearts knoweth what *is* the mind of the Spirit, because he maketh intercession for the saints according to *the will of* God. And we know that **all things work together for good** to them that love God, to them who are the called according to *his* purpose.

For whom he did foreknow, he also did predestinate *to be* conformed to the image of his Son, that he might be the firstborn among many brethren. Moreover whom he did predestinate, them he also called: and whom he called, them he also justified: and whom he justified, them he also glorified.

What shall we then say to these things? **If God *be* for us, who *can be* against us?** He that spared not his own Son, but delivered him up for us all, how shall he not with him also freely give us all things? Who shall lay any thing to the charge of God's elect? *It is* God that justifieth. Who *is* he that condemneth? *It is* Christ that died, yea rather, that is risen again, who is even at the right hand of God, who also maketh intercession for us.

Who shall separate us from the love of Christ? *shall* tribulation, or distress, or persecution, or famine, or nakedness, or peril, or sword? As it is written, For thy sake we are killed all the day long; we are accounted as sheep for the slaughter. Nay, in all these things we are **more than conquerors** through him that loved us. For I am persuaded, that neither death, nor life, nor angels, nor principalities, nor powers, nor things present, nor things to come, Nor height, nor depth, nor any other creature, shall be able to separate us from the love of God, which is in Christ Jesus our Lord. *Romans 8:28-39*

And the God of peace shall **bruise Satan under your feet shortly**. The grace of our Lord Jesus Christ *be* with you. Amen. *Romans 16:20*

Blessed *be* God, even the Father of our Lord Jesus Christ, the Father of mercies, and the God of all comfort; **Who comforteth us in all our tribulation**, that we may be able to comfort them which are in any trouble, by the comfort wherewith we ourselves are comforted of God. For as the sufferings of Christ abound in us, so our consolation also aboundeth by Christ. And whether we be afflicted, *it is* for your consolation and salvation, which is effectual in the enduring of the same sufferings which we also suffer: or whether we be comforted, *it is* for your consolation and salvation.

And our hope of you *is* stedfast, knowing, that as ye are partakers of the sufferings, so *shall ye be* also of the consolation. For we would not, brethren, have you ignorant of our trouble which came to us in Asia, that we were pressed out of measure, above strength, insomuch that we despaired even of life: But we had the sentence of death in ourselves, **that we should not trust in ourselves, but in God** which raiseth the dead: Who delivered us from so great a death, and doth deliver: in whom we trust that he will yet deliver *us*; Ye also helping together by prayer for us, that for the gift *bestowed* upon us by the means of many persons thanks may be given by many on our behalf. *II Corinthians 1:3-11*

And he said unto me, **My grace is sufficient for thee**: for my strength is made perfect in weakness. Most gladly therefore will I rather glory in my infirmities, that the **power of Christ may rest upon me**. Therefore I take pleasure in infirmities, in reproaches, in necessities, in persecutions, in distresses for Christ's sake: **for when I am weak, then am I strong.** *II Corinthians 12:9-10*

Seeing then that **we have a great high priest**, that is passed into the heavens, Jesus the Son of God, let us hold fast *our* profession. For we have not an high priest which cannot be touched with the feeling of our infirmities; but was in all points tempted like as *we are, yet* without sin. Let us therefore come **boldly** unto the throne of grace, that we may **obtain mercy**, and **find grace** to help in time of need. *Hebrews 4:14-16*

My brethren, **count it all joy** when ye fall into divers temptations; Knowing *this*, that the trying of your faith worketh patience. But let patience have *her* perfect work, that ye may be perfect and entire, wanting nothing. *James 1:2-4*

Submit yourselves therefore to God. Resist the devil, and he will flee from you. Draw nigh to God, and he will draw nigh to you. Cleanse *your* hands, *ye* sinners; and purify *your* hearts, *ye* double minded. Be afflicted, and mourn, and weep: let your laughter be turned to mourning, and *your* joy to heaviness. Humble yourselves in the sight of the Lord, and **he shall lift you up.** *James 4:7-10*

Humble yourselves therefore under the mighty hand of God, that he may exalt you **in due time**: **Casting all your care upon him**; for he careth for you.

Be sober, be vigilant; because your adversary the devil, as a roaring lion, walketh about, seeking whom he may devour: Whom resist stedfast in the faith, knowing that the same afflictions are accomplished in your brethren that are in the world.

But the God of all grace, who hath called us unto his eternal glory by Christ Jesus, after that ye have suffered a while, **make you perfect, stablish, strengthen, settle** *you*. To him *be* glory and dominion for ever and ever. Amen. *I Peter 5:6-11*

I Praise God Because He is My…

I PRAISE GOD BECAUSE HE IS MY...

Defense, Fortress, Strong Tower

And he said, **The LORD is my rock**, and my fortress, and my deliverer; The God of my rock; in him will I trust: he is my shield, and the horn of my salvation, my high tower, and my refuge, my saviour; thou savest me from violence. I will call on the LORD, who is **worthy to be praised**: so shall I be saved from mine enemies. *II Samuel 22:2-4*

But thou, O LORD, art **a shield for me**; my glory, and **the lifter up of mine head**. *Psalm 3:3*

My defence is of God, which **saveth the upright in heart**. *Psalm 7:10*

The LORD is my rock, and my fortress, and **my deliverer**; my God, my strength, in whom I will trust; my buckler, and the horn of my salvation, and my high tower. *Psalm 18:2*

The LORD is my strength and my shield; my heart trusted in him, and **I am helped**: therefore my heart greatly rejoiceth; and with my song will I praise him. *Psalm 28:7*

For thou art my rock and my fortress; therefore for thy name's sake lead me, and guide me. *Psalm 31:3*

Because of his strength will I wait upon thee: for God is my defence. *Psalm 59:9*

But I will sing of thy power; yea, I will sing aloud of thy mercy in the morning: for thou hast been my defence and **refuge in the day of my trouble**. Unto thee, O my strength, will I sing: for God is my defence, and **the God of my mercy**. *Psalm 59:16-17*

For thou hast been **a shelter** for me, *and* a strong tower from the enemy. *Psalm 61:3*

He only is my rock and my salvation; he is my defence; **I shall not be greatly moved**. *Psalm 62:2*

Be thou **my strong habitation**, whereunto I may continually resort: thou hast given commandment to save me; for thou art my rock and my fortress. *Psalm 71:3*

For the LORD God is a sun and shield: the LORD **will give grace and glory**: **no good thing will he withhold from them that walk uprightly**. *Psalm 84:11*

For the LORD is our defence; and **the Holy One of Israel is our king**. *Psalm 89:18*

I will say of the LORD, He is my refuge and my fortress: my God; **in him will I trust**. *Psalm 91:2*

But the LORD is my defence; and my God is **the rock of my refuge**. *Psalm 94:22*

Blessed be the LORD my strength, which teacheth my hands to war, and my fingers to fight: My goodness, and my fortress; my high tower, and **my deliverer**; my shield, and he in whom I trust; who subdueth my people under me. *Psalm 144:1-2*

The name of the LORD *is* a strong tower: **the righteous runneth into it, and is safe**. *Proverbs 18:10*

O LORD, my strength, and my fortress, and **my refuge in the day of affliction**, the Gentiles shall come unto thee from the ends of the earth. and shall say, Surely our fathers have inherited lies, vanity, and things wherein there is no profit. *Jeremiah 16:19*

The LORD is good, **a strong hold in the day of trouble**; and he knoweth them that trust in him. *Nahum 1:7*

I PRAISE GOD BECAUSE HE IS MY…

God

The LORD is **my strength and song**, and he is become my salvation: he is my God, and I will prepare him an habitation; my father's God, and **I will exalt him**. *Exodus 15:2*

He is thy praise, and he is thy God, **that hath done for thee these great and terrible things**, which thine eyes have seen. *Deuteronomy 10:21*

In my distress I called upon the LORD, and cried to my God: and **he did hear my voice** out of his temple, and **my cry did enter into his ears**. *II Samuel 22:7*

For by thee I have run through a troop: by my God have I leaped over a wall. For who is God, save the LORD? and who is a rock, save our God? *II Samuel 22:30, 32*

And David said to Solomon his son, **Be strong and of good courage**, and do it: fear not, nor be dismayed: for the LORD God, even my God, will be with thee; **he will not fail thee, nor forsake thee**, until thou hast finished all the work for the service of the house of the LORD. *I Chronicles 28:20*

I know also, my God, that **thou triest the heart**, and hast pleasure in uprightness. As for me, in the uprightness of mine heart I have **willingly offered all these things**: and now have I seen with joy thy people, which are present here, to offer willingly unto thee.
I Chronicles 29:17

And Asa cried unto the LORD, his God, and said, LORD, it is nothing with thee to help, whether with many, or with them that have no power: help us, O LORD our God; for **we rest on thee**, and in thy name we go against this multitude. **O LORD, thou art our God**; let not man prevail against thee. *II Chronicles 14:11*

I was cast upon thee from the womb: thou art **my God from my mother's belly**. *Psalm 22:10*

But **I trusted in thee**, O LORD: I said, Thou art my God. *Psalm 31:14*

Many, O LORD my God, are **thy wonderful works** which thou hast done, and thy thoughts which are to us-ward: they cannot be reckoned up in order unto thee: if I would declare and speak of them, they are **more than can be numbered**. *Psalm 40:5*

Yet the LORD will command his **lovingkindness** in the daytime, and in the night his song shall be with me, and my prayer **unto the God of my life**. *Psalm 42:8*

For this God is our God **for ever and ever**: he will be **our guide** even unto death. *Psalm 48:14*

O God, thou art my God; early will I seek thee: my soul thirsteth for thee, **my flesh longeth for thee** in a dry and thirsty land, where no water is. *Psalm 63:1*

He that is our God is **the God of salvation**; and unto GOD the Lord belong the issues from death. *Psalm 68:20*

I will also praise thee with the psaltery, **even thy truth**, O my God: unto thee will I sing with the harp, O thou Holy One of Israel. *Psalm 71:22*

Yea, the sparrow hath found an house, and the swallow a nest for herself, where she may lay her young, even thine altars, **O LORD of hosts, my King**, and my God. *Psalm 84:3*

For **a day in thy courts** is better than a thousand. I had rather be a doorkeeper in the house of my God, than to dwell in the tents of wickedness. *Psalm 84:10*

I will praise thee, O Lord my God, **with all my heart**: and I will glorify thy name for evermore. *Psalm 86:12*

He shall cry unto me, Thou art **my father**, my God, and the rock of my salvation. *Psalm 89:26*

I will say of the LORD, He is **my refuge and my fortress**: my God; in him will I trust. *Psalm 91:2*

For he is our God; and we are **the people of his pasture**, and the sheep of his hand. Today if ye will hear his voice. *Psalm 95:7*

Bless the LORD, O my soul. O LORD my God, **thou art very great**; thou art **clothed with honour and majesty.** *Psalm 104:1*

I will sing unto the LORD **as long as I live**: I will sing praise to my God while I have my being. *Psalm 104:33*

Thou art my God, and I will praise thee: thou art my God, **I will exalt thee**. *Psalm 118:28*

I will extol thee, my God, O king; and **I will bless thy name** for ever and ever. *Psalm 145:1*

I will say to them which were not my people, Thou art my people; and they shall say, **Thou art my God**. *Isaiah 61:10*

Art thou not from everlasting, O LORD my God, **mine Holy One**? we shall not die. O LORD, thou hast ordained them for judgment; and, O mighty God, thou hast established them for correction. *Habakkuk 1:12*

Jesus saith unto her, Touch me not; for I am not yet ascended to my Father: but go to my brethren, and say unto them, I ascend unto my Father, and **your Father**; and *to* my God, **and your God**. *John 20:17*

And Thomas answered and said unto him, **My Lord and my God**. *John 20:28*

But my God shall supply all your need **according to his riches in glory** by Christ Jesus. *Philippians 4:19*

For our God *is* a **consuming fire**. *Hebrews 12:29*

I WILL PRAISE GOD BECAUSE HE IS MY...

Refuge

The eternal God is thy refuge, and **underneath are the everlasting arms.** *Deuteronomy 33:27*

And he said, The LORD is my rock and my fortress, and **my deliverer;** The God of my rock; **in him will I trust:** he is my shield, and the horn of my salvation, my high tower, and my refuge, my saviour; thou savest me from violence. *II Samuel 22:2-3*

The LORD also will be **a refuge for the oppressed,** a refuge **in times of trouble.** And they that know thy name will put their trust in thee: for thou, LORD, hast not forsaken them that seek thee. *Psalm 9:9-10*

Thou art my **hiding place**; thou shalt preserve me from trouble; thou shalt compass me about with songs of deliverance. *Psalm 32:7*

God is our refuge and strength, **a very present help in trouble.** Therefore will not we fear, though the earth be removed, and though the mountains be carried into the midst of the sea; Though the waters thereof roar and be troubled, though the mountains shake with the swelling thereof. *Psalm 46:1-3*

The LORD of hosts is with us; the God of Jacob is our refuge. *Psalm 46:7*

Be merciful unto me, O God, be merciful unto me: for my soul trusteth in thee: yea, **in the shadow of thy wings** will I make my refuge, until these calamities be overpast. *Psalm 57:1*

But I will sing of thy power; yea, **I will sing aloud of thy mercy in the morning**: for thou hast been my defence and refuge in the day of my trouble. *Psalm 59:16*

In God is my salvation and my glory: the rock of my strength, and my refuge, is in God. Trust in him at all times; ye people, **pour out your heart before him**: God is a refuge for us. *Psalm 62:7-8*

I am as a wonder unto many; but thou art **my strong refuge**. *Psalm 71:7*

I will say of the LORD, He is my refuge and my fortress: my God; **in him will I trust**. *Psalm 91:2*

Because thou hast made the LORD, which is my refuge, even **the most High**, thy habitation; There shall no evil befall thee, neither shall any plague come nigh thy dwelling. *Psalm 91:9-10*

But the LORD is **my defence**; and my God is the rock of my refuge. *Psalm 94:22*

I cried unto thee, O LORD: I said, Thou art my refuge and **my portion** in the land of the living. *Psalm 142:5*

In the fear of the LORD is strong confidence: and **his children** shall have a place of refuge. *Proverbs 14:26*

For thou hast been a strength to the poor, a strength to the needy in his distress, **a refuge from the storm**, a shadow from the heat, when the blast of the terrible ones is as a storm against the wall. *Isaiah 25:4*

O LORD, my strength, and my fortress, and my **refuge in the day of affliction**, the Gentiles shall come unto thee from the ends of the earth, and shall say, Surely our fathers have inherited lies, vanity, and things wherein there is no profit. *Jeremiah 16:19*

I PRAISE GOD BECAUSE HE IS MY...

Rock

For their rock is **not as our Rock**, even our enemies themselves being judges. *Deuteronomy 32:31*

The LORD liveth; and **blessed be my rock**; and exalted be the God of the rock of my salvation. *II Samuel 22:47*

The LORD **liveth**; and blessed *be* my rock; and let the God of my salvation **be exalted**. *Psalm 18:46*

Unto thee will I cry, O LORD my rock; be not silent to me: lest, if thou be silent to me, I become like them that go down into the pit. *Psalm 28:1*

Bow down thine ear to me; **deliver me speedily**: be thou my strong rock, for **an house of defence** to save me. For thou *art* my rock and my fortress; therefore for thy name's sake **lead me**, and guide me. *Psalm 31:2-3*

He **only** *is* my rock and my salvation; *he is* my defence; **I shall not be greatly moved**. *Psalm 62:2*

Be thou **my strong habitation**, whereunto I may **continually** resort: thou hast given commandment to save me; for thou *art* my rock and my fortress. *Psalm 71:3*

To show that the LORD *is* **upright**: *he is* my rock, and *there is* **no unrighteousness** in him. *Psalm 92:15*

I WILL PRAISE GOD BECAUSE HE IS MY...

Salvation

The LORD is my strength and song, and he is **become my salvation**: he is my God, and I will prepare him an habitation; my father's God, and **I will exalt him**. *Exodus 15:2*

The LORD liveth; and blessed be my rock; and exalted be **the God of the rock of my salvation.** *II Samuel 22:47*

Although my house *be* not so with God; yet he hath made with me an everlasting covenant, ordered in all *things*, and sure: for *this is* all my salvation, and **all *my* desire**, although he make *it* not to grow. *II Samuel 23:5*

And say ye, **Save us**, O God of our salvation, and gather us together, and deliver us from the heathen, that we may **give thanks to thy holy name**, *and* **glory in thy praise**. *I Chronicles 16:35*

The LORD liveth; and **blessed *be* my rock**; and let the God of my salvation be exalted. *Psalm 18:46*

Lead me in thy truth, and teach me: for thou *art* the God of my salvation; **on thee do I wait all the day**. *Psalm 25:5*

The LORD is my light and my salvation; whom shall I fear? the LORD **is the strength of my life**; of whom shall I be afraid? *Psalm 27:1*

Make haste to help me, O Lord my salvation. *Psalm 38:22*

Deliver me from bloodguiltiness, O God, thou God of my salvation: and **my tongue shall sing aloud of thy righteousness**. *Psalm 51:14*

By terrible things **in righteousness wilt thou answer us**, O God of our salvation; who art the confidence of all the ends of the earth, and of them that are afar off upon the sea. *Psalm 65:5*

Blessed be the Lord, who daily loadeth us with benefits, even the God of our salvation... He that is our God is the God of salvation; and unto

GOD the Lord belong the issues from death. *Psalm 68:19-20*

Blessed *be* the Lord, *who* **daily loadeth us** *with benefits*, *even* the God of our salvation. *Psalm 68:19*

Help us, O God of our salvation, for the glory of thy name: and **deliver us**, and purge away our sins, for thy name's sake. *Psalm 79:9*

Turn us, O God of our salvation, and cause thine anger toward us to cease. *Psalm 85:4*

O LORD God of my salvation, I have **cried day** *and* **night before thee**. *Psalm 88:1*

He shall cry unto me, **Thou art my father**, my God, and the rock of my salvation. *Psalm 89:26*

O come, let us sing unto the LORD: let us **make a joyful noise** to the rock of our salvation. *Psalm 95:1*

The LORD is **my strength and song**, and is become my salvation. *Psalm 118:14*

Behold, God is my salvation; **I will trust, and not be afraid**: for the LORD JEHOVAH is my strength and my song; he also is become my salvation. *Isaiah 12:2*

O LORD, **be gracious unto us**; we have waited for thee: be thou their arm every morning, our salvation also in the time of trouble. *Isaiah 33:2*

Therefore I will **look unto the LORD**; I will wait for the God of my salvation: my God will hear me. *Micah 7:7*

Yet **I will rejoice** in the LORD, I will joy in the God of my salvation. *Habakkuk 3:18*

I PRAISE GOD BECAUSE HE IS MY…

Strength

The LORD is my strength and song, and he is become my salvation: he is my God, and I will prepare him an habitation; **my father's God**, and I will exalt him. *Exodus 15:2*

God is my strength and power: And he **maketh my way perfect**. *II Samuel 22:33*

I will love thee, O LORD, my strength. The LORD is my rock, and my fortress, and my deliverer; my God, my strength, **in whom I will trust**; my buckler, and the horn of my salvation, and my high tower. *Psalm 18:1-2*

Let the **words of my mouth, and the meditation of my heart**, be acceptable in thy sight, O LORD, my strength, and **my redeemer**. *Psalm 19:14*

But **be not thou far from me**, O LORD: O my strength, haste thee to help me. *Psalm 22:19*

The LORD is my light and my salvation; whom shall I fear? the LORD is the strength of my life; **of whom shall I be afraid**? *Psalm 27:1*

The LORD is my strength and my shield; **my heart trusted in him,** and I am helped: therefore **my heart greatly rejoiceth**; and with my song will I praise him. *Psalm 28:7*

Pull me out of the net that they have laid privily for me: for thou art my strength. *Psalm 31:4*

Unto thee, O my strength, will I sing: for God is my defence, and **the God of my mercy.** *Psalm 59:17*

In God is my salvation and **my glory**: the rock of my strength, and my refuge, is in God. *Psalm 62:7*

Sing aloud unto God our strength: **make a joyful noise** unto the God of

Jacob. *Psalm 81:1*

The LORD is **my strength and song**, and is become my salvation. *Psalm 118:14*

Behold, God is my salvation; **I will trust, and not be afraid**: for the LORD JEHOVAH is my strength and my song; he also is become my salvation. *Isaiah 12:2*

And now, saith the LORD that formed me from the womb *to be* his servant, to bring Jacob again to him, Though Israel be not gathered, yet shall I be glorious in the eyes of the LORD, and **my God shall be my strength**. *Isaiah 49:5*

The LORD God is my strength, and he **will make my feet like hinds' feet**, and he will make me to walk upon mine high places. . . *Habakkuk 3:19*

And he said unto me**, My grace** is sufficient for thee: for **my strength is made perfect in weakness**. Most gladly therefore will I rather glory in my infirmities, that **the power of Christ may rest upon me**. *II Corinthians 12:9*

I Praise God Because He is…

I PRAISE GOD BECAUSE HE IS...

Almighty, Over All

And when Abram was ninety years old and nine, the LORD appeared to Abram, and said unto him, I *am* the Almighty God; **walk before me**, and be thou perfect. *Genesis 17:1*

And God said unto him, **I *am* God Almighty**: be fruitful and multiply; a nation and a company of nations shall be of thee, and kings shall come out of thy loins. *Genesis 35:11*

Even by the God of thy father, who shall help thee; and by the Almighty, **who shall bless thee with blessings of heaven above**, blessings of the deep that lieth under, blessings of the breasts, and of the womb. *Genesis 49:25*

And said, O LORD God of our fathers, *art* not thou God in heaven? and rulest *not* thou over all the kingdoms of the heathen? and in thine hand *is there not* power and might, so that **none is able to withstand thee**? *II Chronicles 20:6*

Shall he that contendeth with the Almighty **instruct *him***? he that reproveth God, let him answer it. *Job 40:2*

For the LORD **most high** *is* terrible; *he is* a great King over all the earth. *Psalm 47:2*

He that dwelleth in the secret place of the most High shall abide under the shadow of the Almighty. *Psalm 91:1*

The LORD hath prepared his throne in the heavens; and **his kingdom ruleth over all**. *Psalm 103:19*

The LORD *is* **good to all**: and **his tender mercies** *are* over all his works. *Psalm 145:9*

And the LORD shall be **king over all the earth**: in that day shall there be one LORD, and his name one. *Zechariah 14:9*

Whose *are* the fathers, and of whom as concerning the flesh Christ *came*, who is over all, **God blessed for ever**. Amen. *Romans 9:5*

For there is no difference between the Jew and the Greek: for **the same Lord** over all is rich unto all that call upon him. *Romans 10:12*

I am Alpha and Omega, **the beginning and the ending**, saith the Lord, which is, and which was, and which is to come, the Almighty. *Revelation 1:8*

And the four beasts had each of them six wings about *him*; and *they were* full of eyes within: and they rest not day and night, saying, **Holy, holy, holy**, Lord God Almighty, which was, and is, and is to come. *Revelation 4:8*

Saying, We give thee thanks, O Lord God Almighty, which art, and wast, and art to come; because thou **hast taken to thee thy great power**, and hast reigned. *Revelation 11:17*

And they sing the song of Moses the servant of God, and the song of the Lamb, saying, **Great and marvellous** *are* **thy works**, Lord God Almighty; **just and true** *are* **thy ways**, thou King of saints. *Revelation 15:3*

And I heard another out of the altar say, Even so, Lord God Almighty, **true and righteous** *are* **thy judgments**. *Revelation 16:7*

And I saw no temple therein: for the Lord God Almighty and the Lamb are **the temple** of it. *Revelation 21:22*

I PRAISE GOD BECAUSE HE IS...

Eternal, Everlasting

And *Abraham* planted a grove in Beersheba, and **called there on the name of the LORD**, the everlasting God. *Genesis 21:33*

Blessed *be* **the LORD God of Israel** from everlasting, and to everlasting. Amen, and Amen. *Psalm 41:13*

Before the mountains were brought forth, or ever thou hadst formed the earth and the world, even from everlasting to everlasting, **thou art God.** *Psalm 90:2*

Thy throne is established of old: thou art from everlasting. *Psalm 93:2*

But the **mercy of the LORD** is from everlasting to everlasting upon them that fear him, and his righteousness unto children's children. *Psalm 103:17*

Blessed *be* the LORD God of Israel **from everlasting to everlasting**: and let all the people say, Amen. Praise ye the LORD. *Psalm 106:48*

Thy righteousness is an **everlasting righteousness**, and thy law is the truth. *Psalm 119:142*

Trust ye in the LORD for ever: for in the LORD JEHOVAH is **everlasting strength.** *Isaiah 26:4*

Hast thou not known? hast thou not heard, that the everlasting God, the LORD, the Creator of the ends of the earth, **fainteth not, neither is weary**? there is **no searching of his understanding**. *Isaiah 40:28*

In a little wrath I hid my face from thee for a moment; but with **everlasting kindness** will I have mercy on thee, saith the LORD thy Redeemer. *Isaiah 54:8*

The sun shall be no more thy light by day; neither for brightness shall the moon give light unto thee: but the LORD shall be unto thee **an everlasting light**, and **thy God thy glory**. Thy sun shall no more go down; neither shall thy moon withdraw itself: for the LORD shall be thine everlasting light, and the days of thy mourning shall be ended. *Isaiah 60:19-20*

Doubtless thou art Our father, though Abraham be ignorant of us, and Israel acknowledge us not: thou, O LORD, art our father, our redeemer; **thy name is from everlasting.** *Isaiah 63:16*

But the LORD is the true God, he is the living God, and **an everlasting king**: at his wrath the earth shall tremble, and the nations shall not be able to abide his indignation. *Jeremiah 10:10*

The LORD hath appeared of old unto me, saying, Yea, I have loved thee with an **everlasting love**: therefore with lovingkindness have I drawn thee. *Jeremiah 31:3*

I blessed the most High, and I praised and honoured him that liveth for ever, whose dominion is an **everlasting dominion**, and his kingdom is from generation to generation. *Daniel 4:34*

Art thou not from everlasting, O LORD my God, **mine Holy One**? we shall not die. O LORD, thou hast ordained them for judgment; and, O mighty God, thou hast established them for correction. *Habakkuk 1:12*

For the invisible things of him from the creation of the world are clearly seen, being understood by the things that are made, even **his eternal power and Godhead**; so that they are without excuse. *Romans 1:20*

But now is made manifest, and by the scriptures of the prophets, according to the commandment of the everlasting God, made known to all nations for the obedience of faith: To **God only wise**, be glory through Jesus Christ for ever. Amen. *Romans 16:26-27*

Now unto the King **eternal, immortal, invisible, the only wise God**, be honour and glory for ever and ever. Amen. *I Timothy 1:17*

But the God of all grace, who hath called us unto his **eternal glory** by Christ Jesus, after that ye have suffered a while, make you perfect, stablish, strengthen, settle you. **To him be glory and dominion for ever and ever.** Amen. *I Peter 5:10-11*

I PRAISE GOD BECAUSE HE IS...

The Father

A father of the fatherless, and a judge of the widows, is God in his holy habitation. *Psalm 68:5*

He shall cry unto me, Thou *art* my father, my God, and the **rock of my salvation**. *Psalm 89:26*

Doubtless thou art our father, though Abraham be ignorant of us, and Israel acknowledge us not: thou, O LORD, art our father, **our redeemer; thy name is from everlasting**. *Isaiah 63:16*

But now, O LORD, **thou art our father; we are the clay, and thou our potter**; and we all are the work of thy hand. *Isaiah 64:8*

Let your light so shine before men, that they may see your good works, and **glorify your Father** which is in heaven. *Matthew 5:16*

Be not ye therefore like unto them: for your Father knoweth what things ye have need of, before ye ask him. After this manner therefore pray ye: **Our Father which art in heaven**. Hallowed be thy name. *Matthew 6:8-9*

Be ye therefore merciful, as **your Father also is merciful**. *Luke 6:36*

If ye then, being evil, know how to give good gifts unto your children: how much more shall **your heavenly Father** give the Holy Spirit to them that ask him? *Luke 11:13*

No man hath seen God at any time; the only begotten Son, **which is in the bosom of the Father**, he hath declared *him. John 1:18*

But the hour cometh, and now is, when the true worshippers shall worship the Father **in spirit and in truth**: for the Father seeketh such to worship him. *John 4:23*

Jesus knowing that the **Father had given all things into his hands**, and that he was come from God, and went to God. *John 13:3*

For **the Father himself loveth you**, because ye have loved me, and have believed that I came out from God. *John 16:27*

Behold, the hour cometh, yea, is now come, that ye shall be scattered, every man to his own, and shall leave me alone: and yet I am not alone, because **the Father is with me**. *John 16:32*

And now, O Father, glorify thou me with thine own self with the glory which I had with thee before the world was. That they all may be one; **as thou, Father, art in me, and I in thee**, that they may also be one in us: that the world may believe that thou hast sent me. *John 17:5, 21*

O righteous Father, the world hath not known thee: but I have known thee, and these have known that thou hast sent me. *John 17:25*

Therefore we are buried with him by baptism into death: that like as Christ was raised up from the dead **by the glory of the Father**, even so we also should walk in newness of life. *Romans 6:4*

For ye have not received the spirit of bondage again to fear; but ye have received the Spirit of adoption, **whereby we cry, Abba, Father.** *Romans 8:15*

That ye may with one mind and one mouth **glorify God, even the Father** of our Lord Jesus Christ. *Romans 15:6*

But to us there is but **one God, the Father, of whom are all things**, and we in him; and one Lord Jesus Christ, by whom are all things, and we by him. *I Corinthians 8:6*

Blessed *be* God, even the Father of our Lord Jesus Christ, **the Father of mercies**, and the God of all comfort. *I Corinthians 1:3*

And because ye are sons, God hath sent forth the Spirit of his Son into your hearts, crying, **Abba, Father.** *Galatians 4:6*

Blessed *be* the God and Father of our Lord Jesus Christ, **who hath blessed us with all spiritual blessings in heavenly** *places* in Christ. *Ephesians 1:3*

That the God of our Lord Jesus Christ, the **Father of glory**, may give unto you the spirit of wisdom and revelation in the knowledge of him. *Ephesians 1:17*

One God and Father of all, who *is* **above all, and through all, and in you all**. *Ephesians 4:6*

Giving thanks always for all things unto God and the Father in the name of our Lord Jesus Christ. *Ephesians 5:20*

And *that* every tongue should confess that Jesus Christ *is* Lord, **to the glory of God the Father.** *Philippians 2:11*

Now unto God and our Father *be* **glory for ever and ever**. Amen. *Philippians 4:20*

That their hearts might be comforted, being knit together in love, and unto all riches of the full assurance of understanding, to the acknowledgement of **the mystery of God**, and of the Father, and of Christ. *Colossians 2:2*

And whatsoever ye do in word or deed, *do* all in the name of the Lord Jesus, **giving thanks to God and the Father by him.** *Colossians 3:17*

Remembering without ceasing your **work of f**aith, and **labour of** love, and **patience of hope** in our Lord Jesus Christ, in the sight of God and our Father. *I Thessalonians 1:3*

Now our Lord Jesus Christ himself, and God, even **our Father, which hath loved us**, and hath given *us* everlasting consolation and good hope through grace. *II Thessalonians 2:16*

If ye endure chastening, God dealeth with you as with sons; for what son is he whom the father chasteneth not? *Hebrews 12:7*

Elect according to **the foreknowledge of God the Father**, through sanctification of the Spirit, unto obedience and sprinkling of the blood of Jesus Christ: Grace unto you, and peace, be multiplied. *I Peter 1:2*

Every good gift and every perfect gift is from above, and cometh down from the **Father of lights**, with whom is no variableness, neither shadow of turning. *James 1:17*

Blessed *be* the God and Father of our Lord Jesus Christ, which according to his abundant mercy hath begotten us again unto a lively hope by the resurrection of Jesus Christ from the dead. *I Peter 1:3*

Behold, **what manner of love** the Father hath bestowed upon us, that we should be called the sons of God: therefore the world knoweth us not, because it knew him not. *I John 3:1*

Grace be with you, mercy, *and* peace, from God the Father, and from the Lord Jesus Christ, the Son of the Father, in truth and love. *II John 1:3*

Jude, the servant of Jesus Christ, and brother of James, to them that are **sanctified by God the Father**, and preserved in Jesus Christ, *and* called. *Jude 1*

And hath made us kings and priests unto God and his Father; **to him *be* glory and dominion for ever and ever.** Amen. *Revelation 1:6*

I PRAISE GOD BECAUSE HE IS...

God

Know therefore this day, and consider it in thine heart, that the **LORD he is God in heaven above, and upon the earth beneath**: there is none else. *Deuteronomy 4:39*

Know therefore that the LORD thy God, he is God, the faithful God, **which keepeth covenant and mercy with them that love him** and keep his commandments to a thousand generations. *Deuteronomy 7:9*

For the LORD your God is God of gods, and Lord of lords, **a great God, a mighty, and a terrible,** which regardeth not persons, nor taketh reward. *Deuteronomy 10:17*

Wherefore thou art great, O LORD God: for there is none like thee, **neither is there any God beside thee**, according to all that we have heard with our ears. *II Samuel 7:22*

For who is God, save the LORD? and who is a rock, save our God? *II Samuel 22:32*

And when all the people saw it, **they fell on their faces**: and they said, The LORD, he is the God; **the LORD, he is the God**. *I Kings 18:39*

And Hezekiah prayed before the LORD, and said, O LORD God of Israel, **which dwellest between the cherubims**, thou art the God, even thou alone, **of all the kingdoms of the earth**; thou hast made heaven and earth. *II Kings 19:15*

O LORD God of our fathers, art not thou God in heaven? and rulest not thou over all the kingdoms of the heathen? and **in thine hand is there not power and might**, so that none is able to withstand thee? *II Chronicles 20:6*

Lead me in thy truth, and teach me: for thou art the God of my salvation; on thee do I wait all the day. *Psalm 25:5*

Be still, and know that I am God: I will be exalted among the heathen, I will be exalted in the earth. *Psalm 46:10*

For this God is **our God for ever and ever**: he will be our guide even unto death. *Psalm 48:14*

He that is our God is the **God of salvation**; and unto GOD the Lord belong the issues from death. *Psalm 68:20*

O God, thou art terrible out of thy holy places: the God of Israel is he that giveth strength and power unto his people. **Blessed be God**. *Psalm 68:35*

Thy way, a God, is in the sanctuary: who is so great a God as our God? Thou art the God that doest wonders: **thou hast declared thy strength** among the people. *Psalm 77:13-14*

My soul longeth, yea, even fainteth for the courts of the LORD: **my heart and my flesh crieth out for the living God.** *Psalm 84:2*

For **thou art great**, and doest **wondrous things**: thou art God alone. *Psalm 86:10*

LORD God of hosts, who is a **strong LORD** like unto thee? or to **thy faithfulness** round about thee? *Psalm 89:8*

For the LORD is a great God, and **a great King above all** gods. *Psalm 95:3*

Know ye that the LORD he is God: it is he that hath made us, and not we ourselves; **we are his people**, and the sheep of his pasture. *Psalm 100:3*

Thou art my God, and **I will praise thee**: thou art my God, I will exalt thee. *Psalm 118:28*

O give thanks unto the **God of gods**: for his mercy endureth for ever. *Psalm 136:2*

Happy is he that hath the God of Jacob for his help, **whose hope is in the LORD his God**. *Psalm 146:5*

Hast thou not known? hast thou not heard, that the everlasting God, the LORD, the **Creator of the ends of the earth**, fainteth not, neither is weary? there is no searching of his understanding. *Isaiah 40:28*

Look unto me, and be ye saved, all the ends of the earth: for I am God, and **there is none else**. *Isaiah 45:22*

But the LORD is **the true God**, he is the living God, and an everlasting king: at his wrath the earth shall tremble, and the nations shall not be able to abide his indignation. *Jeremiah 10:10*

Are there any among the vanities of the Gentiles that can cause rain? or can the heavens give showers? art not thou he, O LORD our God? therefore **we will wait upon thee**: for thou hast made all these things. *Jeremiah 14:22*

Thou shewest lovingkindness unto thousands, and recompensest the iniquity of the fathers into the bosom of their children after them: **the Great, the Mighty God**, the LORD of hosts, is his name. *Jeremiah 32:18*

He is the **living God**, and **stedfast for ever**, and his kingdom that which shall not be destroyed, and his dominion shall be even unto the end. *Daniel 6:26*

For, lo, he that formeth the mountains, and createth the wind, and **declareth unto man what is his thought**, that maketh the morning darkness, and treadeth upon the high places of the earth, The LORD, The God of hosts, is his name. *Amos 4:13*

Blessed be God, even the Father of our Lord Jesus Christ, the Father of mercies, and the **God of all comfort**. *II Corinthians 1:3*

Now unto the **King eternal**, immortal, invisible, the only wise God, be honour and glory for ever and ever. Amen. *I Timothy 1:17*

But the **God of all grace**, who hath called us unto his eternal glory by Christ Jesus, after that ye have suffered a while, make you perfect, stablish, strengthen, settle you. To him be glory and dominion for ever and ever. Amen. *I Peter 5:10-11*

To the **only wise God** our Saviour, be glory and majesty, dominion and power, both now and ever. Amen. *Jude 25*

We give thee thanks, O Lord God Almighty, **which art, and wast, and art to come**; because thou hast taken to thee thy great power, and hast reigned. *Revelation 11:17*

And they sing the song of Moses the servant of God, and the song of the Lamb, saying, Great and **marvellous are thy works**, Lord God Almighty; just and true are thy ways, thou King of saints. *Revelation 15:3*

Alleluia: for the **Lord God omnipotent reigneth**. *Revelation 19:6*

And I heard a great voice out of heaven saying, Behold, the tabernacle of God is with men, and he will dwell with them, and they shall be his people, and **God himself shall be with them**, and be their God. *Revelation 21:3*

I PRAISE GOD BECAUSE HE IS...

Good

O give thanks unto the Lord; for he is good; for his mercy endureth for ever. *I Chronicles 16:34*

And when all the children of Israel saw how **the fire came down, and the glory of the LORD upon the house,** they **bowed themselves with their faces to the ground** upon the pavement, and worshipped, and praised the LORD, saying, For he is good; for his mercy endureth for ever. *II Chronicles 7:3*

And **they sang together** by course in **praising and giving thanks** unto the LORD; because he is good, for his mercy endureth for ever toward Israel. And all the people shouted with a great shout, when they praised the LORD, because the foundation of the house of the LORD was laid. *Ezra 3:11*

Good and upright is the LORD: therefore will he teach sinners in the way. *Psalm 25:8*

O taste and see that the LORD is good: blessed is the man that trusteth in him. *Psalm 34:8*

Hear me, O LORD; for **thy lovingkindness is good**: turn unto me according to the multitude of thy tender mercies. *Psalm 69:16*

For thou, Lord, art good, and ready to forgive; and plenteous in mercy unto all them that call upon thee. *Psalm 86:5*

For the LORD is good; **his mercy is everlasting**; and his truth endureth to all generations. *Psalm 100:5*

But do thou for me, O GOD the Lord, for thy name's sake: because **thy mercy is good**, deliver thou me. *Psalm 109:21*

O give thanks unto the LORD; for he is good: for his mercy endureth for ever. *Psalm 118:29*

Thou art good, and **doest good**; teach me thy statutes. *Psalm 119:68*

Praise the LORD; for the LORD is good: **sing praises unto his name**; for it is pleasant. *Psalm 135:3*

The LORD is good to all: and his tender mercies are over all his works. *Psalm 145:9*

The LORD is good unto them that **wait for him**, to the soul that **seeketh him**. *Lamentations 3:25*

The LORD is good, **a strong hold in the day of trouble**; and he knoweth them that that trust in him. *Nahum 1:7*

How God anointed Jesus of Nazareth with the Holy Ghost and with power: who went about doing good, and **healing all that were oppressed of the devil**; for God was with him. *Acts 10:38*

Or despisest thou the riches of his goodness and forbearance and longsuffering; not knowing that the goodness of God **leadeth thee to repentance**? *Romans 2:4*

Behold therefore **the goodness and severity of God**: on them which fell, severity; but toward thee, goodness, if thou continue in *his* goodness: otherwise thou also shalt be cut off. *Romans 11:22*

Wherefore also we pray always for you, that our God would count you worthy of *this* calling, and **fulfil all the good pleasure of *his* goodness**, and the work of faith with power. *II Thessalonians 1:11*

I PRAISE GOD BECAUSE HE IS…

Great

The LORD your God is God of gods, and a great God, **a mighty, and a terrible**. *Deuteronomy 10:17*

Wherefore thou art great, O LORD God: for *there is* none like thee, **neither *is there any* God beside thee**, according to all that we have heard with our ears. *II Samuel 7:22*

For great *is* the LORD, and **greatly to be praised**: he also *is* to be feared above all gods. *I Chronicles 16:25*

Thine, O LORD, *is* the greatness, and **the power**, and **the glory**, and **the victory**, and the **majesty**: for all *that is* in the heaven and in the earth *is thine*; **thine *is* the kingdom**, O LORD, and thou art **exalted as head above all**. *I Chronicles 29:11*

I beseech thee, O LORD God of heaven, the great and terrible God, **that keepeth covenant and mercy for them that love him** and observe his commandments. *Nehemiah 1:5*

O **how great is thy goodness**, which thou hast laid up for them that fear thee; which thou hast wrought for them that trust in thee before the sons of men! *Psalm 31:19*

For the LORD most high is terrible; he is a **great King over all the earth**. *Psalm 47:2*

Great is the LORD, and **greatly to be praised** in the city of our God, in the mountain of his holiness. *Psalm 48:1*

Say unto God, How terrible art thou in thy works! through **the greatness of thy power** shall thine enemies submit themselves unto thee. *Psalm 66:3*

Thy way, O God, is in the sanctuary: **who is so great a God as our God**? *Psalm 77:13*

For thou art great, and **doest wondrous things**: thou art God alone. *Psalm 86:10*

O LORD, how great are thy works! and **thy thoughts are very deep**. *Psalm 92:5*

For the LORD is **a great God**, and a **great King** above all gods. *Psalm 95:3*

For the LORD is great, and greatly to be praised: he is to be **feared above all gods**. *Psalm 96:4*

The LORD is great in Zion; and he is **high above all the people**. *Psalm 99:2*

For as the heaven is high above the earth, **so great is his mercy** toward them that fear him. *Psalm 103:11*

Bless the LORD, O my soul. O LORD my God, thou art very great; thou art **clothed with and majesty**. *Psalm 104:1*

The works of the LORD are great, sought out them that have pleasure therein. *Psalm 111:2*

The LORD **hath done great things for us**; we are glad. *Psalm 126:3*

For I know that the LORD is great, and that *Our Lord is above all gods*. *Psalm 135:5*

Great is the **glory of the LORD**. *Psalm 138:5*

How precious also are thy thoughts unto me, o God! how great is the sum of them! *Psalm 139:17*

Great is the LORD, and greatly to be praised; and **his greatness is unsearchable**. And men shall speak of the might of thy terrible acts: and I will declare thy greatness. *Psalm 145:3, 6*

Great is our Lord, and of great power: **his understanding is infinite**. *Psalm 147:5*

Praise him for his mighty acts: praise him according to **his excellent greatness.** *Psalm 150:2*

Cry out and shout, thou inhabitant of Zion: **for great is the Holy One of Israel in the midst of thee.** *Isaiah 12:6*

Forasmuch as there is none like unto thee, O LORD; thou art great, and **thy name is great in might.** *Jeremiah 10:6*

Thou shewest loving kindness unto thousands, and recompensest the iniquity of the fathers into the bosom of their children after them: the Great, **the Mighty God, the LORD of hosts**, is his name, **Great in counsel, and mighty in work**: for thine eyes are open upon all the ways of the sons of men: to give every one according to his ways, and according to the fruit of his doings. *Jeremiah 32:18-19*

It is of the LORD'S mercies that we are not consumed, because his compassions fail not. They are new every morning: **great is thy faithfulness.** *Lamentations 3:22-23*

How great are his signs! and how mighty are his wonders! his kingdom is an everlasting kingdom, and his dominion is from generation to generation. *Daniel 4:3*

O Lord, **the great and dreadful God**, keeping the covenant and mercy to them that love him, and to them that keep his commandments. *Daniel 9:4*

The LORD is slow to anger, and **great in power**, and will not at all acquit the wicked: the LORD hath his way in the whirlwind and in the storm, and **the clouds are the dust of his feet.** *Nahum 1:3*

And what is the **exceeding greatness of his power** to us-ward who believe, according to the working of his mighty power. *Ephesians 1:19*

But God, who is rich in mercy, for his great love wherewith he loved us. *Ephesians 2:4*

Ye are of God, little children, and have overcome them: because **greater is he that is in you**, than he that is in the world. *I John 4:4*

Saying, We give thee thanks, O Lord God Almighty, which art, and wast, and art to come; **because thou hast taken to thee thy great power**, and hast reigned. *Revelation 11:17*

And they sing the song of Moses the servant of God, and the song of the Lamb, saying, **Great and marvellous *are* thy works**, Lord God Almighty; **just and true *are* thy ways**, thou King of saints. *Revelation 15:3*

I PRAISE GOD BECAUSE HE IS...

Holy

Speak unto all the congregation of the children of Israel, and say unto them, Ye shall be holy: for **I the LORD your God *am* holy**. *Leviticus 19:2*

There is none holy as the LORD: for ***there is* none beside thee**: neither *is there* any rock like our God. *I Samuel 2:2*

And say ye, Save us, O God of our salvation, and gather us together, and deliver us from the heathen, that we may give thanks to thy holy name, *and* **glory in thy praise**. *I Chronicles 16:35*

But thou art holy, O thou that **inhabitest the praises** of Israel. *Psalm 22:3*

Sing unto the LORD, O ye saints of his, and **give thanks at the remembrance of his holiness**. *Psalm 30:4*

God reigneth over the heathen: God sitteth upon **the throne of his holiness**. *Psalm 47:8*

Great is the LORD, and **greatly to be praised** in the city of our God, in the mountain of his holiness. *Psalm 48:1*

I will also praise thee with the psaltery, *even* **thy truth**, O my God: unto thee will I sing with the harp, O thou Holy One of Israel. *Psalm 71:22*

Thus saith the LORD, **thy Redeemer**, the Holy One of Israel; I *am* the LORD thy God which teacheth thee to profit, which **leadeth thee** by the way *that* thou shouldest go. *Isaiah 48:17*

For the LORD is our defence; and the Holy One of Israel is our king. *Psalm 89:18*

O sing unto the LORD a new song; for he hath done marvellous things: his right hand, and **his holy arm, hath gotten him the victory**. *Psalm 98:1*

Let them **praise thy great and terrible name**; for it is holy. Exalt ye the LORD our God, and **worship at his footstool**; for he is holy. *Psalm 99:3, 5*

Exalt the LORD our God, and **worship at his holy hill**; for the LORD our God *is* holy. *Psalm 99:9*

Bless the LORD, O my soul: and all that is within me, **bless his holy name**. *Psalm 103:1*

Save us, O LORD our God, and gather us from among the heathen, to **give thanks unto thy holy name**, *and* to triumph in thy praise. *Psalm 106:47*

He sent redemption unto his people: he hath commanded his covenant for ever: **holy and reverend is his name**. *Psalm 111:9*

The LORD is righteous in all his ways, and **holy in all his works**. *Psalm 145:17*

But the LORD of hosts shall be exalted in judgment, and God that is holy shall be **sanctified in righteousness**. *Isaiah 5:16*

And one cried unto another, and said, Holy, holy, is the LORD of hosts: **the whole earth is his glory**. *Isaiah 6:3*

Cry out and shout, thou inhabitant of Zion: is the Holy One of Israel **in the midst of thee**. *Isaiah 12:6*

I am the LORD, your Holy One, the creator of Israel, **your King**. *Isaiah 43:15*

Art thou not from everlasting, O LORD **my God, mine Holy One**? we shall not die. O LORD, hast ordained them for judgment; and, Almighty God, thou hast established them for correction. *Habakkuk 1:12*

God came from Teman, and the Holy One from mount Paran. **His glory covered the heavens**, and the **earth was full of his praise**. *Habakkuk 3:3*

For he that is mighty hath done to me great things; and **holy is his name**. *Luke 1:49*

And the four beasts had each of them six wings about *him*; and *they were* full of eyes within: and they rest not day and night, saying, Holy, holy, holy, Lord God Almighty, which **was, and is, and is to come**. *Revelation 4:8*

Who shall not fear thee, O Lord, and glorify thy name? for **thou only art holy**: for all nations shall come and worship before thee; for thy judgments are made manifest. *Revelation 15:4*

I PRAISE GOD BECAUSE HE IS...

Just

He is the Rock, his work *is* perfect: for all his ways *are* judgment: a God of truth and without iniquity, **just and right** *is* **he**. *Deuteronomy 32:4*

Howbeit thou art just in all that is brought upon us; for **thou hast done right**, but we have done wickedly. *Nehemiah 9:33*

Tell ye, and bring *them* near; yea, let them take counsel together: who hath declared this from ancient time? *who* hath told it from that time? *have* not I the LORD? and *there is* no God else beside me; **a just God and a Saviour**; *there is* none beside me. *Isaiah 45:21*

The just LORD *is* in the midst thereof; **he will not do iniquity**: every morning doth he bring his judgment to light, he faileth not; but the unjust knoweth no shame. *Zephaniah 3:5*

And he said, The God of our fathers hath chosen thee, that thou shouldest know his will, and see that **Just One**, and shouldest hear the voice of his mouth. *Acts 22:14*

For Christ also hath once suffered for sins, **the just for the unjust**, that he might bring us to God, being put to death in the flesh, but quickened by the Spirit. *1 Peter 3:18*

If we confess our sins, he is **faithful and just** to forgive us our sins, and to cleanse us from all unrighteousness. *I John 1:9*

And they sing the song of Moses the servant of God, and the song of the Lamb, saying, Great and marvellous *are* thy works, Lord God Almighty; **just and true** *are* **thy ways**, thou King of saints. *Revelation 15:3*

I PRAISE GOD BECAUSE HE IS...

King

The LORD is **King for ever and ever**: the heathen are perished out of his land. *Psalm 10:16*

Lift up your heads, O ye gates; and be ye lift up, ye everlasting doors; and the King of glory shall come in. Who is this **King of glory**? The LORD strong and mighty, the LORD mighty in battle. Lift up your heads, O ye gates; even lift them up, ye everlasting doors; and the King of glory shall come in. Who is this King of glory? The LORD of hosts, he is the King of glory. *Psalm 24:7-10*

For the LORD most high is terrible; he is a **great King over all the earth**. *Psalm 47:2*

Sing praises to God, sing praises: **sing praises unto our King**, sing praises. For God is the King of all the earth: sing ye praises with understanding. *Psalm 47:6-7*

Beautiful for situation, the joy of the whole earth, is mount Zion, on the sides of the north, the city of the great King. *Psalm 48:2*

They have seen thy goings, O God; even **the goings of my God, my King**, in the sanctuary. Psalm 68:24

For God is **my King of old**, working salvation in the midst of the earth. *Psalm 74:12*

Yea, the sparrow hath found an house, and the swallow a nest for herself, where she may lay her young, even thine altars, O LORD of Hosts, **my King, and my God**. *Psalm 84:3*

For the LORD is our defence; and **the Holy One of Israel is our king**. *Psalm 89:18*

For the LORD is a great God, and a **great King above all gods**. *Psalm 95:3*

With trumpets and sound of cornet **make a joyful noise unto the LORD, the King.** *Psalm 98:6*

I will extol thee, my God, O king; and I will bless thy name for ever and ever. *Psalm 145:1*

Let Israel rejoice in him that made him: let the children of Zion **be joyful in their King.** *Psalm 149:2*

Then said I, Woe is me! for I am undone; because I am a man of unclean lips, and I dwell in the midst of a people of unclean lips: for **mine eyes have seen the King**, the LORD of Hosts. *Isaiah 6:5*

For the LORD is **our judge**, the LORD is **our lawgiver**, the LORD is our king; he will save us. *Isaiah 33:22*

I am the LORD, your Holy One, **the creator of Israel, your King.** *Isaiah 43:15*

But the LORD is the true God, he is the living God, and **an everlasting king**: at his wrath the earth shall tremble, and the nations shall not be able to abide his indignation. *Jeremiah 10:10*

Now I **praise and extol and honour the King of heaven**, all whose works are truth, and his ways judgment: and those that walk in pride he is able to abase. *Daniel 4:37*

And the LORD shall be king over all the earth: in that day shall there be one LORD, and his name one. And it shall come to pass, that every one that is left of all the nations which carne against Jerusalem shall even go up from year to year to **worship the King**, the LORD of hosts, and to keep the feast of tabernacles. *Zechariah 14:9, 16*

Saying, **Blessed *be* the King that cometh in the name of the Lord**: peace in heaven, and glory in the highest. *Luke 19:38*

Took branches of palm trees, and went forth to meet him, and cried, **Hosanna**: Blessed *is* the King of Israel that cometh in the name of the Lord. *John 12:13*

Which in his times he shall show, *who is* **the blessed and only Potentate**, the King of kings, and Lord of lords. *II Timothy 6:15*

And they sing the song of Moses the servant of God, and the song of the Lamb, saying, Great and marvellous *are* thy works, Lord God Almighty; just and true *are* thy ways, thou **King of saints.** *Revelation 15:3*

These shall make war with the Lamb, and the Lamb shall overcome them: for he is Lord of lords, and King of kings: and they that are with him *are* **called, and chosen, and faithful**. *Revelation 17:14*

And he hath on *his* vesture and on his thigh a name written, **KING OF KINGS, AND LORD OF LORDS**. *Revelation 19:16*

I PRAISE GOD BECAUSE HE IS...

Lord

Behold, the heaven and the heaven of heavens is the LORD'S thy God, the earth also, with all that therein is. For the LORD your God is God of gods, and Lord of lords, **a great God, a mighty, and a terrible**, which regardeth not persons, nor taketh reward. *Deuteronomy 10:14, 17*

Seek the LORD and his strength, **seek his face continually**. He is the LORD our God; his judgments are in all the earth. *I Chronicles 16:11, 14*

And to stand **every morning** to thank and praise the LORD, and **likewise at even**. *I Chronicles 23:30*

O LORD God of our fathers, art not thou God in heaven? and rulest not thou over all the kingdoms of the heathen? and **in thine hand is there not power and might**, so that none is able to withstand thee? *II Chronicles 20:6*

And when he had consulted with the people, he appointed singers unto the LORD, and that should praise the **beauty of holiness**, as they went out before the army, and to say, Praise the LORD; for his mercy *endureth* for ever. *II Chronicles 20:21*

Then the Levites, Jeshua, and Kadmiel, Bani, Hashabniah, Sherebiah, Hodijah, Shebaniah, *and* Pethahiah, said, **Stand up *and* bless the LORD your God for ever and ever**: and blessed be thy glorious name, which is exalted above all blessing and praise. **Thou, even thou, art LORD alone**; thou hast made heaven, the heaven of heavens, with all their host, the earth, and all things that are therein, the seas, and all that is therein, and thou preservest them all; and the host of heaven worshippeth thee. *Nehemiah 9:5-6*

I will praise the LORD **according to his righteousness**: and will sing praise to the name of the LORD most high. *Psalm 7:17*

O LORD our Lord, **how excellent is thy name** in all the earth! *Psalm 8:9*

I will praise *thee*, O LORD, with my whole heart; I will **show forth all thy marvellous works**. *Psalm 9:1*

The meek shall eat and be satisfied: they shall praise the LORD that **seek him**: your heart shall live for ever. *Psalm 22:26*

The LORD is **my shepherd**; I shall not want. *Psalm 23:1*

Who is this King of glory? **The LORD strong and mighty**, the LORD mighty in battle. Who is this King of glory? The LORD of hosts, he is the King of glory. *Psalm 24:8, 10*

The LORD is **my light and my salvation**; whom shall I fear? the LORD is the strength of my life; of whom shall I be afraid? *Psalm 27:1*

The LORD *is* **my strength and my shield**; my heart trusted in him, and I am helped: therefore my heart greatly rejoiceth; and with my song will I praise him. *Psalm 28:7*

To the end that *my* **glory may sing praise to thee**, and not be silent. O LORD my God, I will give thanks unto thee for ever. *Psalm 30:12*

Rejoice in the LORD, O ye righteous: *for* **praise is comely** for the upright. *Psalm 33:1*

Praise the LORD with harp: sing unto him **with the psaltery** *and* **an instrument of ten strings**. *Psalm 33:2*

Blessed is the nation whose God is the LORD; and the people whom he hath chosen for his own inheritance. *Psalm 33:12*

I will bless the LORD at all times: his praise *shall* **continually** *be* in my mouth. *Psalm 34:1*

And he hath put a new song in my mouth, *even* praise unto our God: **many shall see *it*, and fear**, and shall trust in the LORD. *Psalm 40:3*

So shall the king greatly desire **thy beauty**: for he is thy Lord; and worship thou him. *Psalm 45:11*

For the LORD most high is terrible; he is **a great King over all the earth**. *Psalm 47:2*

O Lord, open thou my lips; and my mouth shall show forth thy praise. *Psalm 51:15*

In God will I praise *his* word: in the LORD **will I praise *his* word**. *Psalm 56:10*

How amiable are thy tabernacles, O LORD of hosts! My soul longeth, yea, even fainteth for the courts of the LORD: **my heart and my flesh crieth out for the living God**. Yea, the sparrow hath found an house, and the swallow a nest for herself, where she may lay her young, even thine altars, O LORD of hosts, my King, and my God. *Psalm 84:1-3*

O LORD of hosts, **blessed** is the man that trusteth in thee. *Psalm 84:12*

I will praise thee, O Lord my God, **with all my heart**: and I will glorify thy name for evermore. *Psalm 86:12*

And the heavens shall praise **thy wonders**, O LORD: **thy faithfulness** also in the congregation of the saints. *Psalm 89:5*

But thou, LORD, art **most high for evermore**. *Psalm 92:8*

Make a joyful noise unto the LORD, all the earth: make a loud noise, and rejoice, and sing praise. *Psalm 98:4*

Know ye that the LORD he is God: it is he that hath made us, and not we ourselves; **we are his people**, and the sheep of his pasture. *Psalm 100:3*

I will sing unto the LORD as long as I live: I will sing praise to my God **while I have my being**. *Psalm 104:33*

Who can utter the mighty acts of the LORD? *who* **can show forth all his praise**? *Psalm 106:2*

Blessed *be* the LORD God of Israel **from everlasting to everlasting**: and let all the people say, Amen. Praise ye the LORD. *Psalm 106:48*

O that *men* would praise the LORD ***for* his goodness,** and *for* his wonderful works to the children of men! *Psalm 107:8*

I will praise thee, O LORD, among the people: and I will sing praises unto thee **among the nations.** *Psalm 108:3*

I will greatly praise the LORD with my mouth; yea, I will praise him among the multitude. *Psalm 109:30*

Praise ye the LORD. Blessed *is* the man *that* **feareth the LORD,** *that* **delighteth greatly** in his commandments. *Psalm 112:1*

The LORD is high above all nations, and **his glory above the heavens.** *Psalm 113:4*

Great is the LORD, and **greatly to be praised**; and his **greatness is unsearchable.** *Psalm 145:3*

But we will bless the LORD **from this time forth and for evermore**. Praise the LORD. *Psalm 115:18*

O praise the LORD, all ye nations: praise him, all ye people. For **his merciful kindness is great** toward us: and the truth of the LORD *endureth* for ever. Praise ye the LORD. *Psalm 117:1-2*

Open to me the gates of righteousness: I will go into them, *and* I will praise the LORD. *Psalm 118:19*

Happy *is that* people, that is in such a case: *yea,* **happy *is that* people,** **whose God** *is* **the LORD**. *Psalm 144:15*

All thy works shall praise thee, O LORD; and thy saints shall bless thee. *Psalm 145:10*

My mouth shall speak the praise of the LORD: and let all flesh bless his holy name for ever and ever. *Psalm 145:21*

Praise ye the LORD. Praise the LORD, **O my soul**. *Psalm 146:1*

While I live will I praise the LORD: I will sing praises unto my God **while I have any being**. *Psalm 146:2*

Sing unto the LORD **with thanksgiving**; sing praise upon the harp unto our God. *Psalm 147:7*

Let them praise the name of the LORD: **for his name alone is excellent**; his glory *is* above the earth and heaven. *Psalm 148:13*

Praise ye the LORD. Sing unto the LORD a new song, *and* **his praise in the congregation of saints**. *Psalm 149:1*

Praise ye the LORD. Praise God **in his sanctuary**: praise him in the firmament of his power. *Psalm 150:1*

Let every thing that hath breath praise the LORD. Praise ye the LORD. *Psalm 150:6*

And in that day shall ye say, Praise the LORD, call upon his name, **declare his doings among the people**, make mention that his name is exalted. *Isaiah 12:4*

O LORD, thou *art* my God; **I will exalt thee**, I will praise thy name; for thou hast done wonderful *things; thy* counsels of old *are* **faithfulness *and* truth**. *Isaiah 25:1*

For the LORD is our **judge**, the LORD is our **lawgiver**, the LORD is our **king**; he will save us. *Isaiah 33:22*

Hast thou not known? hast thou not heard, that **the everlasting God**, the LORD, the Creator of the ends of the earth, fainteth not, neither is weary? there is no searching of his understanding. *Isaiah 40:28*

Sing unto the LORD **a new song**, *and* his praise from the end of the earth, ye that go down to the sea, and all that is therein; the isles, and the inhabitants thereof. *Isaiah 42:10*

To appoint unto them that mourn in Zion, to give unto them beauty for ashes, the oil of joy for mourning, the garment of praise for the spirit of heaviness; that they might be called trees of righteousness, the planting of the LORD, **that he might be glorified**. *Isaiah 61:3*

Heal me, O LORD, and I shall be healed; save me, and I shall be saved: for **thou *art* my praise.** *Jeremiah 17:14*

Blessed is the man that **trusteth in the LORD**, and whose hope the LORD is. *Jeremiah 17:7*

For, lo, he that formeth the mountains, and createth the wind, and declareth unto man what is his thought, that maketh the morning darkness, and treadeth upon the high places of the earth, The LORD, **The God of hosts**, is his name. *Amos 4:13*

But the LORD is **in his holy temple**: let all the earth keep silence before him. *Habakkuk 2:20*

For I am the LORD, **I change not**. *Malachi 3:6*

Which in his times he shall shew, who is **the blessed and only Potentate**, the King of kings, and Lord of lords. *I Timothy 6:15*

Thou art worthy, O Lord, to receive glory and honour and power: for thou hast created all things, and for thy pleasure they are and were created. *Revelation 4:11*

We give thee thanks, O Lord God Almighty, which art, and wast, and art to come; because thou hast taken to thee thy great power, and hast reigned. *Revelation 11:17*

And they sing the song of Moses the servant of God, and the song of the Lamb, saying, Great and marvellous are thy works, **Lord God Almighty**; just and true are thy ways, thou King of saints. Who shall not fear thee, O Lord, and glorify thy name? for thou only art holy: for all nations shall come and worship before thee; for thy judgments are made manifest. *Revelation 15:3-4*

Alleluia: for the **Lord God omnipotent** reigneth. *Revelation 19:6*

I PRAISE GOD BECAUSE HE IS...

Love

He brought me to the banqueting house, and **his banner over me was love**. *Song of Solomon 2:4*

Behold, for peace I had great bitterness; but thou hast **in love to my soul delivered it from the pit** of corruption: for thou hast cast all my sins behind thy back. *Isaiah 38:17*

Yea, I have loved thee with **an everlasting love**: therefore with lovingkindness have I drawn thee. *Jeremiah 31:3*

The LORD thy God in the midst of thee *is* mighty; he will save, he will rejoice over thee with joy; **he will rest in his love**, he will joy over thee with singing. *Zephaniah 3:17*

But woe unto you, Pharisees! for ye tithe mint and rue and all manner of herbs, and pass over judgment and **the love of God**: these ought ye to have done, and not to leave the other undone. *Luke 11:42*

And hope maketh not ashamed; because the love of God is **shed abroad in our hearts** by the Holy Ghost which is given unto us. *Romans 5:5*

But God **commendeth his love toward us**, in that, while we were yet sinners, Christ died for us. *Romans 5:8*

For I am persuaded, that neither death, nor life, nor angels, nor principalities, nor powers, nor things present, nor things to come, nor height, nor depth, nor any creature, shall be able to separate us from the **love of God, which is in Christ Jesus our Lord**. *Romans 8:38-39*

Now I beseech you, brethren, for the Lord Jesus Christ's sake, and for the **love of the Spirit**, that ye strive together with me in *your* prayers to God for me. *Romans 15:30*

Finally, brethren, farewell. Be perfect, be of good comfort, be of one mind, live in peace; and **the God of love and peace shall be with you**. *II Corinthians 13:11*

The **grace** of the Lord Jesus Christ, and the **love** of God, and the **communion** of the Holy Ghost, *be* with you all. Amen. *II Corinthians 13:14*

But God, who is rich in mercy, for **his great love** wherewith he loved us, Even when we were dead in sins, hath quickened us together with Christ, (by grace ye are saved.) *Ephesians 2:4-5*

And to **know the love of Christ**, which passeth knowledge, that ye might be filled with all the fulness of God. *Ephesians 3:19*

Peace *be* to the brethren, and **love with faith**, from God the Father and the Lord Jesus Christ. *Ephesians 6:23*

And the Lord **direct your hearts into the love of God**, and into the patient waiting for Christ. *II Thessalonians 3:5*

For God hath not given us the spirit of fear; but of **power**, and of **love**, and of a **sound mind**. *II Timothy 1:7*

But after that **the kindness and love** of God our Saviour toward man appeared. *Titus 3:4*

But whoso keepeth his Word, in him verily is **the love of God perfected**: hereby know we that we are in him. *I John 2:5*

Behold, what manner of **love the Father** hath bestowed upon us, that we should be called the sons of God: therefore the world knoweth us not, because it knew him not. *I John 3:1*

Hereby perceive we the love *of God*, because **he laid down his life for us**: and we ought to lay down *our* lives for the brethren. *I John 3:16*

Beloved, let us love one another: for **love is of God**; and everyone that loveth is born of God, and knoweth God. He that loveth not knoweth not God; for **God is love**. In this was manifested the love of God toward us, because that God sent his only begotten Son into the world, that we might live through him. Herein is love, not that we loved God, but that **he loved us**, and sent his Son to be the propitiation for our sins. *I John 4:7-10*

And we have **known and believed the love that God hath to us**. God is love; and he that dwelleth in love dwelleth in God, and God in him. *I John 4:16*

Grace be with you, mercy, *and* peace, from God the Father, and from the Lord Jesus Christ, the Son of the Father, **in truth and love**. *II John 1:3*

Keep yourselves in the love of God, looking for the mercy of our Lord Jesus Christ unto eternal life. *Jude 21*

I PRAISE GOD BECAUSE HE IS…

Merciful

And the LORD passed by before him, and proclaimed, The LORD, The LORD God, merciful and gracious, **longsuffering**, and **abundant in goodness and truth**. *Exodus 34:6*

(For the LORD thy God *is* a merciful God;) he will not forsake thee, neither destroy thee, **nor forget the covenant of thy fathers which he sware unto them**. *Deuteronomy 4:31*

With the merciful thou wilt show thyself merciful, *and* with the upright man thou wilt show thyself upright. *II Samuel 22:26*

For if ye turn again unto the LORD, your brethren and your children *shall find* compassion before them that lead them captive, so that they shall come again into this land: for the LORD your God *is* gracious and merciful, and **will not turn away** *his* **face from you**, if ye return unto him. *II Chronicles 30:9*

And refused to obey, neither were mindful of thy wonders that thou didst among them; but hardened their necks, and in their rebellion appointed a captain to return to their bondage: but thou *art* a God **ready to pardon**, gracious and merciful, slow to anger, and of great kindness, and forsookest them not. *Nehemiah 9:17*

Nevertheless **for thy great mercies' sake thou didst not utterly consume them**, nor forsake them; for thou *art* a gracious and merciful God. *Nehemiah 9:31*

With the merciful thou wilt show thyself merciful; with an upright man thou wilt show thyself upright. *Psalm 18:25*

The LORD *is* merciful and gracious, slow to anger, and **plenteous in mercy**. *Psalm 103:8*

Gracious *is* the LORD, and **righteous**; yea, our God *is* merciful. *Psalm 116:5*

For his merciful kindness is **great toward us**: and the truth of the LORD *endureth* for ever. Praise ye the LORD. *Psalm 117:2*

Let, I pray thee, **thy merciful kindness** be for my comfort, according to thy word unto thy servant. *Psalm 119:76*

Go and proclaim these words toward the north, and say, Return, thou backsliding Israel, saith the LORD; *and* I will not cause mine anger to fall upon you: **for I *am* merciful**, saith the LORD, *and* I will not keep *anger* for ever. *Jeremiah 3:12*

And rend your heart, and not your garments, and turn unto the LORD your God: for he *is* gracious and merciful, **slow to anger**, and of great kindness, and repenteth him of the evil. *Joel 2:13*

And he prayed unto the LORD, and said, I pray thee, O LORD, *was* not this my saying, when I was yet in my country? Therefore I fled before unto Tarshish: for I knew that thou *art* **a gracious God, and merciful**, slow to anger, and of great kindness, and repentest thee of the evil. *Jonah 4:2*

Be ye therefore merciful, **as your Father also is merciful.** *Luke 6:36*

Wherefore in all things it behoved him to be made like unto *his* brethren, that he might be a **merciful and faithful high priest** in things *pertaining* to God, to make reconciliation for the sins of the people. *Hebrews 2:17*

For I will be merciful **to their unrighteousness**, and their sins and their iniquities will I remember no more. *Hebrews 8:12*

I PRAISE GOD BECAUSE HE IS...

Mighty

But his bow abode in strength, and the arms of **his hands were made strong** by the hands of the mighty *God* of Jacob; (from thence *is* the shepherd, the stone of Israel). *Genesis 49:24*

Thou shalt not be affrighted at them: for the LORD thy God *is* among you, **a mighty God and terrible.** *Deuteronomy 7:21*

And know ye this day: for I speak not with you children which have not known, and which have no seen chastisement of the LORD your God, **his mighty hand**, and his stretched out arm. *Deuteronomy 11:2*

Now therefore, our God, **the great, the mighty**, and the terrible God, who keepest covenant and mercy, let not all the trouble seem little before thee that hath come upon us. *Nehemiah 9:32*

Who is this King of glory? The LORD **strong and mighty**, the LORD mighty in battle. *Psalm 24:8*

To him that rideth upon the heavens of heavens, which were of old; lo, he doth send out his voice, and that **a mighty voice.** *Psalm 68:33*

Thou hast a mighty arm: **strong is thy hand, and high is thy right hand,** *Psalm 89:13*

Who can utter **the mighty acts** of the LORD? who can shew forth all his praise? *Psalm 106:2*

One generation shall praise thy works to another, and shall declare thy **mighty acts.** *Psalm 145:4*

Praise him for his mighty acts: praise him according to his excellent greatness. *Psalm 150:2*

Lift up your eyes on high, and behold who hath created these *things*, that bringeth out their host by number: he calleth them all by names by the **greatness of his might,** for that *he is* strong in power; not one faileth. *Isaiah 40:26*

Thou showest lovingkindness unto thousands, and recompensest the iniquity of the fathers into the bosom of their children after them: the Great, the Mighty God, **the LORD of hosts,** *is* his name. *Jeremiah 32:18*

Blessed be the name of God for ever and wisdom and might are his. *Daniel 2:20*

How great are his signs! and how **mighty are his wonders**! his kingdom is an everlasting kingdom, dominion is from generation to generation. *Daniel 4:3*

***Art* thou not from everlasting**, O LORD my God, mine **Holy One**? we shall not die. O LORD, thou hast ordained them for judgment; and, O mighty God, thou hast established them for correction. *Habakkuk 1:12*

The LORD **thy God in the midst of thee is mighty**; he will save, he will rejoice over thee with joy; he will rest in his love, he will joy over thee with singing. *Zephaniah 3:17*

For he that is mighty hath done to me great things; and holy is his name. *Luke 1:49*

And what is the exceeding greatness of his power to us-ward who believe, according to the **working of his mighty power**. *Ephesians 1:19*

I PRAISE GOD BECAUSE HE IS...

Patient, Longsuffering

And the LORD passed by before him, and proclaimed, The LORD, The LORD God, merciful and gracious, longsuffering, and **abundant in goodness and truth**. *Exodus 34:6*

The LORD *is* longsuffering, and **of great mercy**, forgiving iniquity and transgression, and by no means clearing *the guilty*, visiting the iniquity of the fathers upon the children unto the third and fourth *generation. Numbers 14:18*

But thou, O LORD, art a God full of **compassion and gracious**, longsuffering, and **plenteous in mercy and truth**. *Psalm 86:15*

O LORD, **thou knowest: remember me**, and visit me, and revenge me of my persecutors; take me not away in thy longsuffering: know that for thy sake I have suffered rebuke. *Jeremiah 15:15*

Or despisest thou the riches of his goodness and forbearance and longsuffering; not knowing that **the goodnesss of God leadeth thee to repentance.** *Romans 2:4*

Now the God of **patience and consolation** grant you to be likeminded one toward another according to Christ Jesus. *Romans 15:5*

But the **fruit of the Spirit** is love, joy, peace, **longsuffering**, gentleness, goodness, faith. *Galatians 5:22*

Howbeit for this cause I obtained mercy, that in me first Jesus Christ might **show forth all longsuffering**, for a pattern to them which should hereafter believe on him to life everlasting. *I Timothy 1:16*

Which sometime were disobedient, when once **the longsuffering of God waited in the days of Noah**, while the ark was a preparing, wherein few, that is, eight souls were saved by water. *I Peter 3:20*

The Lord is not slack concerning his promise, as some men count slackness; but is longsuffering to us-ward, **not willing that any should perish**, but that all should come to repentance. *II Peter 3:9*

And account *that* the longsuffering of our Lord *is* **salvation**; even as our beloved brother Paul also according to the wisdom given unto him hath written unto you. *II Peter 3:15*

I PRAISE GOD BECAUSE HE IS...

Righteous

O LORD God of Israel, **thou art righteous**: for we remain yet escaped, as it is this day: behold, we are before thee in our trespasses: for we cannot stand before thee because of this. *Ezra 9:15*

O let the wickedness of the wicked come to an end; but establish the just: for the righteous God **trieth the hearts and reins.** *Psalm 7:9*

For **the righteous LORD loveth righteousness**; his countenance doth behold the upright. *Psalm 11:7*

The fear of the LORD is clean, enduring for ever: **the judgments of the LORD are true** and righteous altogether. *Psalm 19:9*

Gracious is the LORD, and righteous; yea, our God is merciful. *Psalm 116:5*

Righteous art thou, O LORD, and **upright are thy judgments**. Thy testimonies that thou hast commanded are righteous and **very faithful**. *Psalm 119:137-138*

The LORD is righteous **in all his ways**, and holy in all his works. *Psalm 145:17*

Therefore hath the LORD watched upon the evil, and brought it upon us: for the LORD Our God is **righteous in all his works** which he doeth: for we obeyed not his voice. *Daniel 9:14*

Henceforth there is laid up for me a crown of righteousness, which the Lord, **the righteous judge**, shall give me at that day: and not to me only, but unto all them also that **love his appearing**. *II Timothy 4:8*

If ye know that he is righteous, ye know that **every one that doeth righteousness is born of him**. *I John 2:29*

Little children, let no man deceive you: **he that doeth righteousness is righteous**, even as he is righteous. *I John 3:7*

And I heard the angel of the waters say, Thou art righteous, O Lord, which art, and wast, and shalt be, **because thou hast judged thus**. *Revelation 16:5*

For **true and righteous** are his judgments. *Revelation 19:2*

I PRAISE GOD BECAUSE HE IS...

Unique, None Like Him

And he said, To morrow. And he said, *Be it* according to thy word: **that thou mayest know** that *there is* none like unto the LORD our God. *Exodus 8:10*

Who *is* like unto thee, O LORD, among the gods? who *is* like thee, **glorious in holiness**, **fearful *in* praises**, **doing wonders**? *Exodus 15:11*

There is none like unto the God of Jeshurun, *who* **rideth upon the heaven in thy hel**p, and in **his excellency** on the sky. *Deuteronomy 33:26*

Wherefore thou art great, O LORD God: **for *there is* none like thee**, neither *is there any* God beside thee, according to all that we have heard with our ears. *II Samuel 7:22*

O LORD, *there is* none like thee, **neither *is there any* God beside** thee, according to all that we have heard with our ears. *I Chronicles 17:20*

Among the gods *there is* none like unto thee, O Lord; neither *are there any works* like unto thy works. *Psalm 86:8*

Who *is* like unto the LORD our God, **who dwelleth on high**, Who humbleth *himself* to behold *the things that are* in heaven, and in the earth! *Psalm 113:5-6*

Remember the former things of old: for **I** *am* **God, and** *there is* **none else**; *I am* God, and *there is* none like me. *Isaiah 46:9*

Forasmuch as *there is* none like unto thee, O LORD; **thou *art* great, and thy name *is* great in might**. *Jeremiah 10:6*

Who would not fear thee, O King of nations? for to thee doth it appertain: forasmuch as among all the wise *men* of the nations, and in all their kingdoms, *there is* none like unto thee. *Jeremiah 10:7*

I PRAISE GOD BECAUSE HE IS...

Wise

O the depth of the riches both of the wisdom and knowledge of God! how unsearchable *are* his judgments, and his ways past finding out! *Romans 11:33*

To God only wise, *be* glory through Jesus Christ for ever. Amen. *Romans 16:27*

For after that **in the wisdom of God the world by wisdom knew not God**, it pleased God by the foolishness of preaching to save them that believe. *I Corinthians 1:21*

But unto them which are called, both Jews and Greeks, **Christ the power of God**, and **the wisdom of God.** *I Corinthians 1:24*

Because the foolishness of God is wiser than men; and the weakness of God is stronger than men. *I Corinthians 1:25*

But God hath chosen the foolish things of the world to **confound the wise**; and God hath chosen the weak things of the world to confound the things which are mighty. *I Corinthians 1:27*

But we speak **the wisdom of God in a mystery**, *even* **the hidden wisdom**, which God ordained before the world unto our glory. *I Corinthians 2:7*

To the intent that now unto the principalities and powers in heavenly *places* might be known by the church **the manifold wisdom of God.** *Ephesians 3:10*

Now unto the King **eternal, immortal, invisible**, the only wise God, *be* honour and glory for ever and ever. Amen. *I Timothy 1:17*

If any of you lack wisdom, let him ask of God, that **giveth to all** *men* **liberally**, and upbraideth not; and it shall be given him. *James 1:5*

To the only wise God our Saviour, *be* **glory and majesty, dominion and power**, both now and for ever. Amen. *Jude 25*

I Praise God for His…

I PRAISE GOD FOR HIS...

Beauty

Give unto the LORD the glory *due* unto his name: bring an offering, and come before him: **worship the LORD in the beauty of holiness**. *I Chronicles 16:29*

And when he had consulted with the people, he appointed singers unto the LORD, and that should **praise the beauty of holiness**, as they went out before the army, and to say, Praise the LORD; for his mercy *endureth* for ever. *II Chronicles 20:21*

One *thing* have I desired of the LORD, that will I seek after; that I may dwell in the house of the LORD all the days of my life, **to behold the beauty of the LORD**, and to inquire in his temple. *Psalm 27:4*

Give unto the LORD **the glory due unto his name**; worship the LORD in the beauty of holiness. *Psalm 29:2*

Out of Zion, **the perfection of beauty**, God hath shined. *Psalm 50:2*

And let the beauty of the LORD our God be upon us: and establish thou the work of our hands upon us; yea, the work of our hands establish thou it. *Psalm 90:17*

Honour and majesty *are* before him: **strength and beauty *are* in his sanctuary**. *Psalm 96:6*

O worship the LORD in the beauty of holiness: **fear before him, all the** earth. *Psalm 96:9*

Thy people *shall be* willing in **the day of thy power**, in the beauties of holiness from the womb of the morning: thou hast the dew of thy youth. *Psalm 110:3*

In that day shall the branch of the LORD be **beautiful and glorious**, and the fruit of the earth *shall be* excellent and comely for them that are escaped of Israel. *Isaiah 4:2*

In that day shall the LORD of hosts be for a crown of glory, and for a **diadem of beauty**, unto the residue of his people. *Isaiah 28:5*

Thine eyes shall **see the king in his beauty**: they shall behold the land that is very far off. *Isaiah 33:17*

I PRAISE GOD FOR HIS...

Faithfulness

Thy mercy, O LORD, *is* in the heavens; *and* **thy faithfulness *reacheth* unto the clouds.** *Psalm 36:5*

I have not hid thy righteousness within my heart; **I have declared thy faithfulness and thy salvation**: I have not concealed thy lovingkindness and thy truth from the great congregation. *Psalm 40:10*

I will sing of the mercies of the LORD for ever: **with my mouth will I make known** thy faithfulness to all generations. For I have said, Mercy shall be built up for ever: **thy faithfulness shalt thou establish in the very heavens.** *Psalm 89:1-2*

And the heavens shall **praise thy wonders**, O LORD: thy faithfulness also in the congregation of the saints. *Psalm 89:5*

O LORD God of hosts, who *is* **a strong LORD** like unto thee? or to thy faithfulness round about thee? *Psalm 89:8*

To show forth thy lovingkindness in the morning, and **thy faithfulness every night.** *Psalm 92:2*

Thy faithfulness *is* unto all generations: thou hast established the earth, and it abideth. *Psalm 119:90*

Hear my prayer, O LORD, give ear to my supplications: **in thy faithfulness answer me**, *and* in thy righteousness. *Psalm 143:1*

They are new every morning: **great *is* thy faithfulness.** *Lamentations 3:23*

O LORD, thou art my God; I will exalt thee, I will praise thy name; for thou hast done wonderful things; thy counsels of old are **faithfulness and truth.** *Isaiah 25:1*

I WILL PRAISE GOD FOR HIS...

Glory

And the sight of the glory of the LORD was like **devouring fire** on the top of the mount in the eyes of the children of Israel. *Exodus 24:17*

Declare his glory among the heathen; his works among all nations. Glory and honour are in his presence; and gladness are in his place. Give unto the LORD, ye kindreds of the people, give unto the LORD glory and strength. Give unto the LORD the glory due unto his name: bring an offering and come before him: worship the LORD in the beauty of holiness. *I Chronicles 16:24, 27-29*

Now when Solomon had made an end of praying, the fire came down from heaven, and consumed the burnt offering and the sacrifices; and **the glory of the LORD filled the** house. And the priests could not enter into the house of the LORD, because the glory of the LORD had filled the LORD'S house. And when all the children of Israel saw how **the fire came down**, and the glory of the LORD upon the house, they bowed themselves with their faces to the ground upon the pavement, and worshipped, and praised the LORD, *saying*, For *he is* good; for his mercy *endureth* for ever. Then the king and all the people offered sacrifices before the LORD. *II Chronicles 7:1-4*

O LORD our Lord, how excellent is thy name in all the earth! **who hast set thy glory above the heavens.** *Psalm 8:1*

The heavens declare the glory of God; and the firmament sheweth his handywork. *Psalm 19:1*

In his temple doth every one speak of his glory. *Psalm 29:9*

O GOD, thou art my God; early will I seek thee: my soul thirsteth for thee, my flesh longeth for thee in a dry and thirsty land, where no water is; **To see thy power and thy glory**, so as I have seen thee in the sanctuary. *Psalm 63:1-2*

And blessed *be* his glorious name for ever: and **let the whole earth be filled *with* his glory**; Amen, and Amen. *Psalm 72:19*

The heavens declare his righteousness, and **all the people see his glory**. *Psalm 97:6*

Yea, they shall sing in the ways of the LORD: for **great is the glory of the LORD**. *Psalm 138:5*

In that day shall the LORD of hosts be for **a crown of glory**, and for a diadem of beauty, unto the residue of his people. *Isaiah 28:5*

Arise, shine; for thy light is come, and **the glory of the LORD is risen upon thee**. For, behold, the darkness shall cover the earth and gross darkness the people: but the LORD shall arise upon thee, and his glory shall be seen upon thee. *Isaiah 60:1-2*

The sun shall be no more thy light by day; neither for brightness shall the moon give light unto thee: but the LORD shall be unto thee **an everlasting light**, and thy God thy glory. *Isaiah 60:19*

Then the glory of the LORD went up from the cherub, and stood over the threshold of the house; and the house was filled with the cloud, and **the court was full of the brightness of the LORD'S glory**. *Ezekiel 10:4*

And, behold, the glory of the God of Israel came from the way of the east: and his voice was like a noise of many waters: and **the earth shined with his glory**. So the spirit took me up, and brought me into the inner court; and, behold, the glory of the LORD filled the house. *Ezekiel 43:2, 5*

God came from Teman, and the Holy One from mount Paran. *Selah* **His glory covered the heavens**, and the earth was full of his praise. *Habakkuk 3:3*

But Peter and they that were with him were heavy with sleep: and when they were awake, they **saw his glory**, and the two men that stood with him. *Luke 9:32*

And the Word was made flesh, and dwelt among us, (and we beheld his glory, **the glory as of the only begotten of the Father**,) full of grace and truth. *John 1:14*

But he, being full of the Holy Ghost, looked up stedfastly into heaven, and **saw the glory of God**, and Jesus standing on the right hand of God. *Acts 7:55*

For God, who commanded the light to shine out of darkness, hath shined in our hearts, to *give* the light of the knowledge of **the glory of God in the face of Jesus Christ**. *II Corinthians 4:6*

That he would grant you, according to **the riches of his glory**, to be strengthened with might by his Spirit in the inner man. *Ephesians 3:16*

Who being **the brightness of *his* glory**, and the express image of his person, and upholding all things by the word of his power, when he had by himself purged our sins, sat down on the right hand of the Majesty on high. *Hebrews 1:3*

But we see Jesus, who was made a little lower than the angels for the suffering of death, **crowned with glory and honour**; that he by the grace of God should taste death for every man. *Hebrews 2:9*

But the God of all grace, who hath called us unto **his eternal glory by Christ Jesus**, after that ye have suffered a while, make you perfect, stablish, strengthen, settle *you. I Peter 5:10*

Now unto him that is able to keep you from falling, and to present *you* faultless before the **presence of his glory** with exceeding joy. *Jude 24*

And the city had no need of the sun, neither moon, to shine in it: for **the glory of God did lighten it**, and the Lamb is the light thereof. *Revelation 21:23*

I PRAISE GOD FOR HIS...

Grace

And it shall come to pass, when he crieth unto me, that I will hear; for **I am gracious**. *Exodus 22:27*

Nevertheless for thy great mercies' sake thou didst not utterly consume them, nor forsake them; for thou art a **gracious and merciful God**. *Nehemiah 9:31*

For the LORD God is a sun and shield: the LORD will give grace and glory: no good thing will he withhold from them that walk uprightly. *Psalm 84:11*

But thou, O LORD, art a God **full of compassion**, and gracious, longsuffering, and plenteous in mercy and truth. *Psalm 86:15*

He hath made his wonderful works to be remembered: the LORD is gracious and full of compassion. *Psalm 111:4*

Unto the upright there ariseth **light in the darkness**: he is gracious, and full of compassion, and righteous. *Psalm 112:4*

Gracious is the LORD and righteous; yea, **our God is merciful**. *Psalm 116:5*

And therefore will the LORD wait, that he may be gracious unto you, and therefore will he be exalted, that he may have mercy upon you: for is a God of judgment: **blessed are all wait for him**. For the people shall dwell in Zion at Jerusalem: thou shalt weep no more: he will be gracious unto thee **at the voice of thy cry**; when he shall hear it, he will answer thee. *Isaiah 30:18-19*

And rend your heart, and not your garments, and turn unto the LORD your God: for he is gracious and merciful, **slow to anger, and of great kindness**, and repenteth him of the evil. *Joel 2:13*

And the Word was made flesh, and dwelt among us, (and we beheld his glory, the glory as of the only begotten of the Father,) **full of grace and truth**. *John 1:14*

And of his fulness have all we received, and **grace for grace**. *John 1:16*

For the law was given by Moses, *but* **grace and truth came by Jesus Christ**. *John 1:17*

And with great power gave the apostles witness of the resurrection of the Lord Jesus: and **great grace was upon them all**. *Acts 4:33*

Long time therefore abode they speaking boldly in the Lord, which gave testimony unto the word of his grace, and **granted signs and wonders** to be done by their hands. *Acts 14:3*

And now, brethren, I commend you to God, and **to the word of his grace**, which is able to build you up, and to give you an inheritance among all them which are sanctified. *Acts 20:32*

Being **justified freely by his grace** through the redemption that is in Christ Jesus. *Romans 3:24*

By whom also we have access by faith into **this grace wherein we stand**, and rejoice in hope of the glory of God. *Romans 5:2*

For if by one man's offence death reigned by one; much more they which receive **abundance of grace** and of the gift of righteousness shall reign in life by one, Jesus Christ.) *Romans 5:17*

For sin shall not have dominion over you: for **ye are not under the law**, but under grace. *Romans 6:14*

For ye know the grace of our Lord Jesus Christ, that, though he was rich, yet **for your sakes he became poor**, that ye through his poverty might be rich. *II Corinthians 8:9*

And God *is* able to **make all grace abound toward you**; that ye, always having all sufficiency in all *things*, may abound to every good work. *II Corinthians 9:8*

And by their prayer for you, which long after you for **the exceeding grace of God** in you. *II Corinthians 9:14*

And he said unto me, **My grace is sufficient for thee**: for my strength is made perfect in weakness. Most gladly therefore will I rather glory in my infirmities, that the power of Christ may rest upon me. *II Corinthians 12:9*

To the praise of the glory of his grace, wherein he hath made us accepted in the beloved. In whom we have redemption through his blood, the forgiveness of sins, according to **the riches of his grace.** *Ephesians 1:6-7*

That in the ages to come he might show **the exceeding riches of his grace** in *his* kindness toward us through Christ Jesus. For **by grace are ye saved through faith**; and that not of yourselves: *it is* the gift of God. *Ephesians 2:7-8*

Now our Lord Jesus Christ himself, and God, even our Father, which hath loved us, and hath given *us* **everlasting consolation and good hope** through grace. *II Thessalonians 2:16*

Who hath saved us, and called *us* with an holy calling, not according to our works, but according to **his own purpose and grace**, which was given us in Christ Jesus before the world began. *II Timothy 1:9*

Thou therefore, my son, **be strong in the grace that is in Christ Jesus**. *II Timothy 2:1*

For the grace of God that bringeth salvation **appeared to all men**. *Titus 2:11*

That being **justified by his grace**, we should be made heirs according to the hope of eternal life. *Titus 3:7*

Let us therefore come boldly unto **the throne of grace**, that we may obtain mercy, and find grace to help in time of need. *Hebrews 4:16*

But he giveth more grace. Wherefore he saith, God resisteth the proud, but **giveth grace unto the humble.** *James 4:6*

As every man hath received the gift, even so minister the same one to another, as good stewards of **the manifold grace of God.** *I Peter 4:10*

But the **God of all grace**, who hath called us unto his eternal glory by Christ Jesus, after that ye have suffered a while, make you perfect, stablish, strengthen, settle you. *I Peter 5:10*

But **grow in grace**, and *in* the knowledge of our Lord and Saviour Jesus Christ. To him *be* glory both now and for ever. Amen. *II Peter 3:18*

I PRAISE GOD FOR HIS...

Lovingkindness

Shew thy marvellous lovingkindness, O thou that savest by thy right hand them which put their trust in thee from those that rise up against them. *Psalm 17:7*

Remember, O LORD, thy tender mercies and thy lovingkindnesses; for **they have been ever of old.** *Psalm 25:6*

For thy lovingkindness *is* before mine eyes: and I have walked in thy truth. *Psalm 26:3*

How excellent *is* thy lovingkindness, O God! therefore the children of men put their trust under the shadow of thy wings. *Psalm 36:7*

O continue thy lovingkindness unto them that know thee; and thy righteousness to the upright in heart. *Psalm 36:10*

I have not hid thy righteousness within my heart; I have declared thy faithfulness and thy salvation: **I have not concealed thy lovingkindness and thy truth** from the great congregation. Withhold not thou thy tender mercies from me, O LORD: let thy lovingkindness and thy truth continually preserve me. *Psalm 40:10-11*

Yet **the LORD will command his lovingkindness in the daytime**, and in the night his song shall be with me, and my prayer unto the God of my life. *Psalm 42:8*

We have thought of thy lovingkindness, O God, in the midst of thy temple. *Psalm 48:9*

Have mercy upon me, O God, **according to thy lovingkindness**: according unto the multitude of thy tender mercies blot out my transgressions. *Psalm 51:1*

Because **thy lovingkindness *is* better than life**, my lips shall praise thee. *Psalm 63:3*

Hear me, O LORD; for **thy lovingkindness *is* good**: turn unto me according to the multitude of thy tender mercies. *Psalm 69:16*

It is a good thing to give thanks unto the LORD, and to sing praises unto thy name, O most High: To shew forth thy lovingkindness in the morning, and thy faithfulness every night. *Psalm 92:1-2*

Bless the LORD, O my soul, and **forget not all his benefits**: Who **forgiveth all thine iniquities**; who **healeth all thy diseases**; Who **redeemeth thy life from destruction**; who **crowneth thee** with lovingkindness and **tender mercies**. *Psalm 103:2-4*

Whoso is wise, and will observe these things, **even they shall understand the lovingkindness of the LORD**. *Psalm 107:43*

Quicken me after thy lovingkindness; so shall **I keep the testimony of thy mouth**. *Psalm 119:88*

Hear my voice according unto thy lovingkindness: O LORD, quicken me according to thy judgment. *Psalm 119:149*

Consider how I love thy precepts: **quicken me**, O LORD, according to thy lovingkindness. *Psalm 119:159*

I will worship toward thy holy temple, and **praise thy name for thy lovingkindness** and for thy truth: for thou hast magnified thy word above all thy name. *Psalm 138:2*

Cause me to hear thy lovingkindness in the morning; for in thee do I trust: cause me to know the way wherein I should walk; for I lift up my soul unto thee. *Psalm 143:8*

I will mention the lovingkindnesses of the LORD, and the praises of the LORD, according to all that the LORD hath bestowed on us, and the great goodness toward the house of Israel, which he hath bestowed on them according to his mercies, and according to **the multitude of his lovingkindnesses**. *Isaiah 63:7*

But let him that glorieth glory in this, that he understandeth and knoweth me, that I am the LORD which **exercise lovingkindness**, judgment, and righteousness, in the earth: for in these things I delight, saith the LORD. *Jeremiah 9:24*

Yea, I have loved thee with an everlasting love: therefore with **lovingkindness I have drawn thee**. *Jeremiah 31:3*

Thou shewest lovingkindness unto thousands, and recompensest the iniquity of the fathers into the bosom of their children after them: the Great, the Mighty God, the LORD of hosts is his name. *Jeremiah 32:18*

I PRAISE GOD FOR HIS...

Majesty

Thine, O LORD, *is* **the greatness, and the power, and the glory, and the victory**, and the majesty: for all *that is* in the heaven and in the earth *is thine*; thine *is* the kingdom, O LORD, and thou art exalted as head above all. *1 Chronicles 29:11*

The voice of the LORD is powerful; **the voice of the LORD is full of majesty.** *Psalm 29:4*

Gird thy sword upon *thy* thigh, O *most* mighty, with **thy glory and thy majesty.** And in thy majesty ride prosperously because of truth and meekness *and* righteousness; and thy right hand shall teach thee terrible things. *Psalm 45:3-4*

The LORD reigneth, he is **clothed with majesty**; the LORD is clothed with strength, wherewith he hath girded himself: the world also is stablished, that it cannot be moved. *Psalm 93:1*

Honour and majesty are before him: strength and beauty are in his sanctuary. *Psalm 96:6*

Bless the LORD, O my soul. O LORD my God, **thou art very great**; thou art clothed with honour and majesty. Psalm *104:1*

I will speak of **the glorious honour of thy majesty**, and of thy wondrous works. *Psalm 145:5*

Enter into the rock, and hide thee in the dust, **for fear of the LORD**, and for the glory of his majesty. *Isaiah 2:10*

To go into the clefts of the rocks, and into the tops of the ragged rocks, for fear of the LORD, and for **the glory of his majesty**, when he ariseth to shake terribly the earth. *Isaiah 2:21*

They shall lift up their voice, **they shall sing for the majesty of the LORD**, they shall cry aloud from the sea. *Isaiah 24:14*

And he shall stand and feed in the strength of the LORD, in **the majesty of the name of the LORD** his God; and they shall abide: for now shall he be great unto the ends of the earth. *Micah 5:4*

Now of the things which we have spoken this is the sum: We have such an high priest, who is set on the right hand of **the throne of the Majesty in the heavens**. *Hebrews 8:1*

For we have not followed cunningly devised fables, when we made known unto you the power and coming of our Lord Jesus Christ, but were **eyewitnesses of his majesty**. *II Peter 1:16*

I PRAISE GOD FOR HIS…

Mercy

Thou in thy mercy **hast led forth the people** *which* **thou hast redeemed**: thou hast guided *them* in thy strength unto thy holy habitation. *Exodus 15:13*

O give thanks unto the LORD; for he is good; for **his mercy endureth for ever.** *I Chronicles 16:34*

Yet thou in **thy manifold mercies** forsookest them not in the wilderness: the pillar of the cloud departed not from them by day, to lead them in the way; neither the pillar of fire by night, to shew them light, and the way wherein they should go. *Nehemiah 9:19*

But as for me, I will come *into* thy house in **the multitude of thy mercy**: *and* in thy fear will I worship toward thy holy temple. *Psalm 5:7*

But **I have trusted in thy mercy**; my heart shall rejoice in thy salvation. *Psalm 13:5*

Remember not the sins of my youth, nor my transgressions: **according to thy mercy remember thou me** for thy goodness' sake, O LORD. *Psalm 25:7*

I will be glad and rejoice in thy mercy: for thou hast considered my trouble; thou hast known my soul in adversities. *Psalm 31:7*

Behold, the eye of the LORD *is* upon them that fear him, upon them that **hope in his mercy.** *Psalm 33:18*

But I will sing of thy power; yea, **I will sing aloud of thy mercy in the morning**: for thou hast been my defence and refuge in the day of my trouble. *Psalm 59:16*

Blessed *be* God, which **hath not turned away my prayer**, nor his mercy from me. *Psalm 66:20*

I will praise thee, O Lord my God, with all my heart: and I will glorify thy name for evermore. **For great is thy mercy toward me**: and thou hast delivered my soul from the lowest hell. But thou, O Lord, art a God full of compassion, and gracious, longsuffering, and **plenteous in mercy and truth**. *Psalm 86:12-13, 15*

I will sing of the mercies of the LORD for ever: with my mouth will I make known thy faithfulness to all generations. *Psalm 89:1*

When I said, My foot slippeth; **thy mercy, O LORD, held me up**. *Psalm 94:18*

For the LORD *is* good; **his mercy *is* everlasting**; and his truth *endureth* to all generations. *Psalm 100:5*

But the mercy of the LORD *is* **from everlasting to everlasting upon them that fear him**, and his righteousness unto children's children. *Psalm 103:17*

But do thou for me, O GOD the Lord, for thy name's sake: because **thy mercy is good**, deliver thou me. *Psalm 109:21*

For **his merciful kindness is great toward us**: and the truth of the LORD endureth for ever. Praise ye the LORD. *Psalm 117:2*

The earth, O LORD, is full of thy mercy: teach me thy statutes. *Psalm 119:64*

Let Israel hope in the LORD: for **with the LORD *there is* mercy**, and with him *is* plenteous redemption. *Psalm 130:7*

O give thanks unto the **God of gods**: for his mercy *endureth* for ever. O give thanks to the **Lord of lords**: for his mercy *endureth* for ever. *Psalm 136:2-3*

The LORD is gracious, and full of compassion; slow to anger, and of great mercy. The LORD is good to all: and **his tender mercies are over all his works**. *Psalm 145:8-9*

Sing, O heavens; and be joyful, O earth; and break forth into singing, O mountains: for the LORD hath comforted his people, and **will have mercy upon his afflicted**. *Isaiah 49:13*

In a little wrath I hid my face from thee for a moment; but **with everlasting kindness** will I have mercy on thee, saith the LORD thy Redeemer. *Isaiah 54:8*

Who *is* a God like unto thee, that pardoneth iniquity, and passeth by the transgression of the remnant of his heritage? he retaineth not his anger for ever, because **he delighteth *in* mercy**. *Micah 7:18*

And **his mercy *is* on them that fear him** from generation to generation. *Luke 1:50*

Through the tender mercy of our God; **whereby the dayspring from on high hath visited us.** *Luke 1:78*

And that the Gentiles might **glorify God for *his* mercy**; as it is written, For this cause I will confess to thee among the Gentiles, and sing unto thy name. *Romans 15:9*

Blessed be God, even the Father of our Lord Jesus Christ, the **Father of mercies**, and the God of all comfort. *II Corinthians 1:3*

But God, who is **rich in mercy**, for his great love wherewith he loved us, Even when we were dead in sins, hath quickened us together with Christ, (by grace ye are saved). *Ephesians 2:4-5*

Not by works of righteousness which we have done, but **according to his mercy he saved us**, by the washing of regeneration, and renewing of the Holy Ghost. *Titus 3:5*

But the wisdom that is from above is first pure, then peaceable, gentle, and easy to be entreated, **full of mercy** and good fruits, without partiality, and without hypocrisy. *James 3:17*

Behold, we count them happy which endure. Ye have heard of the patience of Job, and have seen the end of the Lord; that the Lord is very pitiful, and of **tender mercy**. *James 5:11*

Blessed *be* the God and Father of our Lord Jesus Christ, which according to **his abundant mercy** hath begotten us again unto a lively hope by the resurrection of Jesus Christ from the dead. *I Peter 1:3*

Which in time past *were* not a people, but *are* now the people of God: which had not obtained mercy, but **now have obtained mercy.** *I Peter 2:10*

I PRAISE GOD FOR HIS...

Name

Therefore I will give thanks unto thee, O LORD, among the heathen, and **I will sing praises unto thy name**. *II Samuel 22:50*

Glory ye in his holy name: let the heart of them rejoice that seek the LORD. *I Chronicles 16:10*

Give unto the LORD the **glory due unto his name**: bring an offering, and come before him: worship the LORD in the beauty of holiness. *I Chronicles 16:29*

And say ye, Save us, O God of our salvation, and gather us together, and deliver us from the heathen, that we may **give thanks to thy holy name**, and glory in thy praise. *I Chronicles 16:35*

Stand up and bless the LORD your God for ever and ever: and **blessed be thy glorious name**, which is exalted above all blessing and praise. *Nehemiah 9:5*

The LORD gave and the LORD hath taken away; **blessed be the name of the LORD**. *Job 1:21*

But let all those that put their trust in thee rejoice: let them ever shout for joy, because thou defendest them: **let them also that love thy name be joyful in thee**. *Psalm 5:11*

I will praise the LORD according to his righteousness: and **will sing praise to the name of the LORD most high**. *Psalm 7:17*

O LORD our Lord, **how excellent is thy name** in all the earth! who hast set thy glory above the heavens. *Psalm 8:1*

Give unto the LORD **the glory due unto his name**; worship the LORD in the beauty of holiness. *Psalm 29:2*

For our heart shall rejoice in him, because **we have trusted in his holy name**. *Psalm 33:21*

O magnify the LORD with me, and let us exalt his name together. *Psalm 34:3*

In God we boast all the day long, and praise thy name for ever. *Psalm 44:8*

I will make thy name to be remembered in all generations: therefore shall the people praise thee for ever and ever. *Psalm 45:17*

According to thy name, O God, so *is* thy praise unto the ends of the earth: thy right hand is full of righteousness. *Psalm 48:10*

I will praise thee for ever, because thou hast done *it*: and **I will wait on thy name**; for *it is* good before thy saints. *Psalm 52:9*

I will freely sacrifice unto thee: I will praise thy name, O LORD; for ***it is* good**. *Psalm 54:6*

So will I sing praise unto thy name for ever, **that I may daily perform my vows**. *Psalm 61:8*

Thus will I bless thee while I live: **I will lift up my hands in thy name**. *Psalm 63:4*

Sing forth the honour of his name: make his praise glorious. All the earth shall worship thee, and shall sing unto thee; they shall sing to thy name. *Psalm 66:2, 4*

Sing unto God, sing praises to his name: extol him that rideth upon the heavens **by his name JAH**, and rejoice before him. *Psalm 68:4*

I will praise the name of God with a song, and **will magnify him with thanksgiving**. *Psalm 69:30*

His name shall endure for ever: his name shall be continued as long as the sun: and men shall be blessed in him: all nations shall call him blessed. And blessed be his glorious name for ever: and let the whole earth be filled with his glory; Amen, and Amen. *Psalm 72:17, 19*

Unto thee, a God, do we give thanks, unto thee do we give thanks: for that **thy name is near** thy wondrous works declare. *Psalm 75:1*

Teach me thy way, O LORD; I will walk in thy truth: **unite my heart to fear thy name**. I will praise thee, O LORD my God, with all my heart: and I will glorify thy name for evermore. *Psalm 86:11-12*

Sing unto the LORD, bless his name; **show forth his salvation from day to day**. *Psalm 96:2*

Give unto the LORD **the glory due unto his name**: bring an offering, and come into his courts. *Psalm 96:8*

Let them praise **thy great and terrible name**; for it is holy. *Psalm 99:3*

Enter into his gates with thanksgiving, *and* into his courts with praise: be thankful unto him, *and* **bless his name**. *Psalm 100:4*

Bless the LORD, O my soul: and all that is within me, **bless his holy name**. *Psalm 103:1*

Glory ye in his holy name: let the heart of them rejoice that seek the LORD. *Psalm 105:3*

He sent redemption unto his people: he hath commanded his covenant for ever: **holy and reverend is his name**. *Psalm 111:9*

From the rising of the sun unto the going down of the same the LORD'S name is to be praised. *Psalm 113:3*

Our help is in the name of the LORD, who made heaven and earth. *Psalm 124:8*

Praise the LORD; for the LORD *is* good: sing praises unto his name; for *it is* **pleasant**. *Psalm 135:3*

I will worship toward thy holy temple, and praise thy name for thy lovingkindness and for thy truth: for **thou hast magnified thy word above all thy name**. *Psalm 138:2*

I will extol thee, my God, O king; and I will bless thy name for ever and ever. Every day will I bless thee; and I will praise thy name for ever and ever. *Psalm 145:1-2*

My mouth shall speak the praise of the LORD: and **let all flesh bless his holy name** for ever and ever. *Psalm 145:21*

Let them praise the name of the LORD: **for he commanded, and they were created**. *Psalm 148:5*

Let them praise the name of the LORD: for **his name alone is excellent**; his glory is above the earth and heaven. *Psalm 148:13*

Let them praise his name in the dance: let them sing praises unto him with the timbrel and harp. *Psalm 149:3*

And in that day shall ye say, Praise the LORD, call upon his name, declare his doings among the people, **make mention that his name is exalted**. *Isaiah 12:4*

O LORD, thou *art* my God; I will exalt thee, I will praise thy name; for **thou hast done wonderful *things*;** *thy* counsels of old *are* faithfulness *and* truth. *Isaiah 25:1*

Saying, **I will declare thy name unto my brethren**, in the midst of the church will I sing praise unto thee. *Hebrews 2:12*

By him therefore let us offer the **sacrifice of praise to God continually**, that is, **the fruit of *our* lips giving thanks to his name.** *Hebrews 13:15*

I PRAISE GOD FOR HIS...

Power

Be thou exalted, LORD, in thine own strength: *so* **will we sing and praise thy power.** *Psalm 21:13*

But **I will sing of thy power**; yea, I will sing aloud of thy mercy in the morning: for thou hast been my defence and refuge in the day of my trouble. *Psalm 59:16*

To see **thy power and thy glory**, so *as* I have seen thee in the sanctuary. *Psalm 63:2*

Say unto God, How terrible *art thou in* thy works! through **the greatness of thy power** shall thine enemies submit themselves unto thee. *Psalm 66:3*

He ruleth by his power for ever; his eyes behold the nations: let not the rebellious exalt themselves. *Psalm 66:7*

Now also when I am old and greyheaded, O God, forsake me not; until I have showed thy strength unto *this* generation, *and* **thy power to every one *that* is to come.** *Psalm 71:18*

Let the sighing of the prisoner come before thee; according to **the greatness of thy power** preserve thou those that are appointed to die. *Psalm 79:11*

Thy people *shall be* willing in **the day of thy power**, in the beauties of holiness from the womb of the morning: thou hast the dew of thy youth. *Psalm 110:3*

They shall speak of the glory of thy kingdom, and **talk of thy power**. *Psalm 145:11*

Praise ye the LORD. Praise God in his sanctuary: praise him in **the firmament of his power**. *Psalm 150:1*

He hath made the earth by his power, he hath established the world by his wisdom, and hath stretched out the heaven by his understanding. *Jeremiah 51:15*

And *his* brightness was as the light; he had horns *coming* out of his hand: and there *was* **the hiding of his power**. *Habakkuk 3:4*

And what *is* the exceeding greatness of his power to us-ward who believe, according to **the working of his mighty power**. *Ephesians 1:19*

Whereof I was made a minister, according to the gift of the grace of God given unto me by **the effectual working of his power**. *Ephesians 3:7*

Who being the brightness of *his* glory, and the express image of his person, and **upholding all things by the word of his power**, when he had by himself purged our sins, sat down on the right hand of the Majesty on high. *Hebrews 1:3*

And the temple was filled with smoke **from the glory of God**, and from his power; and no man was able to enter into the temple, till the seven plagues of the seven angels were fulfilled. *Revelation 15:8*

I PRAISE GOD FOR HIS…

Righteousness

In thee, O LORD, do I put my trust; let me never be ashamed: **deliver me in thy righteousness.** *Psalm 31:1*

Thy righteousness *is* like the great mountains; thy judgments *are* a great deep: O LORD, thou preservest man and beast. *Psalm 36:6*

O continue thy lovingkindness unto them that know thee; and **thy righteousness to the upright in heart.** *Psalm 36:10*

I have not hid thy righteousness within my heart; **I have declared** thy faithfulness and thy salvation: I have not concealed thy lovingkindness and thy truth from the great congregation. *Psalm 40:10*

Deliver me from bloodguiltiness, O God, thou God of my salvation: *and* **my tongue shall sing aloud of thy righteousness.** *Psalm 51:14*

Deliver me in thy righteousness, and cause me to escape: incline thine ear unto me, and save me. *Psalm 71:2*

My mouth shall show forth thy righteousness *and* thy salvation all the day; for I know not the numbers *thereof. Psalm 71:15*

I will go in the strength of the Lord GOD: I will m**ake mention of thy righteousness, *even* of thine only**. *Psalm 71:16*

Thy righteousness also, O God, *is* **very high**, who hast done great things: O God, who *is* like unto thee! *Psalm 71:19*

My tongue also shall **talk of thy righteousness all the day long**: for they are confounded, for they are brought unto shame, that seek my hurt. *Psalm 71:24*

In thy name shall they rejoice all the day: and in thy righteousness shall they be exalted. *Psalm 89:16*

Behold, I have longed after thy precepts: **quicken me in thy righteousness.** *Psalm 119:40*

Mine eyes fail for thy salvation, and for **the word of thy righteousness**. *Psalm 119:123*

Thy righteousness *is* **an everlasting righteousness**, and thy law *is* the truth. *Psalm 119:142*

Hear my prayer, O LORD, give ear to my supplications: in thy faithfulness **answer me,** *and* **in thy righteousness.** *Psalm 143:1*

They shall abundantly utter the memory of thy great goodness, and **shall sing of thy righteousness.** *Psalm 145:7*

I will **declare thy righteousness, and thy works**; for they shall not profit thee. *Isaiah 57:12*

Then shall thy light break forth as the morning, and thine health shall spring forth speedily: and **thy righteousness shall go before thee**; the glory of the LORD shall be thy reward. *Isaiah 58:8*

And **the Gentiles shall see thy righteousness**, and all kings thy glory: and thou shalt be called by a new name, which the mouth of the LORD shall name. *Isaiah 62:2*

But **seek ye first the kingdom of God, and his righteousness**; and all these things shall be added unto you. *Matthew 6:33*

Whom God hath set forth *to be* a propitiation through faith in his blood, to declare his righteousness **for the remission of sins that are past**, through the forbearance of God. *Romans 3:25*

To declare, *I say*, at this time **his righteousness**: that he might be just, and the justifier of him which believeth in Jesus. *Romans 3:26*

As it is written, He hath dispersed abroad; he hath given to the poor: **his righteousness remaineth for ever.** *II Corinthians 9:9*

I PRAISE GOD FOR HIS...

Word

Blessed *be* the LORD, that hath given rest unto his people Israel, according to a**ll that he promised: t**here hath not failed one word of all his good promise, which he promised by the hand of Moses his servant. *I Kings 8:56*

As for God, his way *is* perfect: **the word of the LORD is tried**: he *is* a buckler to all those that trust in him. *Psalm 18:30*

For the word of the LORD *is* right; and all his works *are done* in **truth. By the word of the LORD were the heavens made**; and all the host of them by the breath of his mouth. *Psalm 33:4, 6*

In God I will praise his word, in God I have put my trust; I will not fear what flesh can do unto me. *Psalm 56:4*

He sent his word, and **healed them**, and delivered *them* from their destructions. *Psalm 107:20*

Thy word have **I hid in mine heart**, that I might not sin against thee. *Psalm 119:11*

I will delight myself in thy statutes: **I will not forget** thy word. *Psalm 119:16*

My soul melteth for heaviness: strengthen thou me according unto thy word. *Psalm 119:28*

So shall I have wherewith to answer him that reproacheth me: for **I trust in thy word**. *Psalm 119:42*

I entreated thy favour with *my* whole heart: **be merciful unto me according to thy word**. *Psalm 119:58*

My soul fainteth for thy salvation: *but* **I hope in thy word**. *Psalm 119:81*

For ever, O LORD, **thy word is settled in heaven.** *Psalm 119:89*

Thy word *is* **a lamp unto my feet**, and a light unto my path. *Psalm 119:105*

Thou *art* my hiding place and my shield: I hope in thy word. *Psalm 119:114*

Thy word *is* very pure: therefore thy servant loveth it. *Psalm 119:140*

Thy word *is* true *from* the beginning: and every one of thy righteous judgments *endureth* for ever. *Psalm 119:160*

I rejoice at thy word, as one that findeth great spoil. *Psalm 119:162*

My tongue shall speak of thy word: for all thy commandments *are* righteousness. *Psalm 119:172*

I will worship toward thy holy temple, and praise thy name for thy lovingkindness and for thy truth: for **thou hast magnified thy word above all thy name**. *Psalm 138:2*

Every word of God *is* pure: he *is* a shield unto them that put their trust in him. *Proverbs 30:5*

The grass withereth, the flower fadeth: but the word of our God shall **stand for ever**. *Isaiah 40:8*

So shall my word be that goeth forth out of my mouth: it shall not return unto me void, but **it shall accomplish that which I please**, and it shall prosper *in the thing* whereto I sent it. *Isaiah 55:11*

Thy words were found, and I did eat them; and **thy word was unto me the joy and rejoicing of mine heart:** for I am called by thy name, O LORD God of hosts. *Jeremiah 15:16*

Sanctify them through thy truth: **thy word is truth**. *John 17:17*

So then **faith cometh by hearing**, and hearing by the word of God. *Romans 10:17*

And take the helmet of salvation, and **the sword of the Spirit**, which is the word of God. *Ephesians 6:17*

For the word of God is **quick, and powerful**, and sharper than any two-edged sword, piercing even to the dividing asunder of soul and spirit, and of the joints and marrow, and is **a discerner of the thoughts and intents of the heart**. *Hebrews 4:12*

Through faith we understand that **the worlds were framed by the word of God**, so that things which are seen were not made of things which do appear. *Hebrews 11:3*

Being born again, not of corruptible seed, but of incorruptible, by the word of God, which liveth and abideth for ever. For all flesh is as grass, and all the glory of man as the flower of grass. The grass withereth, and the flower thereof falleth away: But **the word of the Lord endureth for ever**. And this is the word which by the gospel is preached unto you. *I Peter 1:23-25*

I Praise God Because He…

I PRAISE GOD BECAUSE HE...

Delivers

He **delivereth and rescueth**, and he worketh signs and wonders in heaven and in earth, who hath delivered Daniel from the power of the lions. *Daniel 6:27*

But the LORD your God ye shall fear; and **he shall deliver you out of the hand of all your enemies**. *II Kings 17:39*

And say ye, Save us, O God of our salvation, and gather us together, and deliver us from the heathen**, that we may give thanks to thy holy name, *and* glory in thy** praise. *I Chronicles 16:35*

The LORD *is* **my rock, and my fortress, and my deliverer**; my God, my strength, in whom I will trust; my buckler, and the horn of my salvation, *and* my high tower. *Psalm 18:2*

He delivered me from my strong enemy, and from them which hated me: for they were too strong for me. He brought me forth also into a large place; he delivered me, because he delighted in me. *Psalm 18:17, 19*

He delivereth me from mine enemies: yea, **thou liftest me up above those that rise up against me**: thou hast delivered me from the violent man. *Psalm 18:48*

Our fathers trusted in thee: they trusted, and thou didst deliver them. They cried unto thee, and were delivered: they trusted in thee, and were not confounded. *Psalm 22:4-5*

Thou art my hiding place; thou shalt preserve me from trouble; thou shalt compass me about **with songs of deliverance**. *Psalm 32:7*

I sought the LORD, and he heard me, and **delivered me from all my fears**. *Psalm 34:4*

The righteous cry, and the LORD heareth, and **delivereth them out of all their troubles**. Many are the afflictions of the righteous: but the LORD delivereth him out of them all. *Psalm 34:17, 19*

The LORD shall help them, and deliver shall deliver them from the wicked, and **because they trust in him.** *Psalm 37:40*

But I *am* poor and needy; *yet* the Lord thinketh upon me: thou *art* **my help and my deliverer**; make no tarrying, O my God. *Psalm 40:17*

And call upon me in the day of trouble: I thee, and **thou shalt glorify me.** *Psalm 50:15*

For thou hast delivered my soul from death: *wilt* not *thou deliver* **my feet from falling**, that I may walk before God in the light of the living? *Psalm 56:13*

Great is thy mercy toward me: and thou hast delivered **my soul from the lowest hell.** *Psalm 86:13*

Because he hath set his love upon me, therefore will I deliver him: I will set him on high, because he hath known my name. He shall call upon me, and I will answer him: **I will be with him in trouble**; I will deliver him, and honour him. *Psalm 91:14-15*

He sent his word, and healed them, and delivered them from their destructions. *Psalm 107:20*

For thou hast delivered my soul from death, **mine eyes from tears, and my feet from falling.** *Psalm 116:8*

Who delivered us **from so great a death**, and doth deliver: in whom we trust that he will yet deliver us. *II Corinthians 1:10*

Who hath delivered us **from the power of darkness**, and hath translated us into the kingdom of his dear Son. *Colossians 1:13*

Persecutions, afflictions, which came unto me at Antioch, at Iconium, at Lystra; what I endured: but out of them all the Lord delivered me. *II Timothy 3:11*

And the Lord shall deliver me from every evil work, and will preserve me unto his heavenly kingdom: **to whom be glory for ever and ever**. *II Timothy 4:18*

Lord **knoweth how** to deliver the godly out of temptations, and to reserve the unjust for the day of judgment to be punished. *II Peter 2:9*

I PRAISE GOD BECAUSE HE...

Does Wonders

Who *is* like unto thee, O LORD, among the gods? who *is* like thee, glorious in holiness, fearful *in* praises, doing wonders? *Exodus 15:11*

And Joshua said unto the people, **Sanctify yourselves**: for to morrow the LORD will do wonders among you. *Joshua 3:5*

Sing unto him, sing psalms unto him, talk ye of all his wondrous works. *I Chronicles 16:9*

Remember his marvellous works that he hath done, **his wonders**, and the judgments of his mouth. *I Chronicles 16:12*

That I may publish **with the voice of thanksgiving**, and tell of all thy wondrous works. *Psalm 26:7*

Many, O LORD my God, *are* thy wonderful works *which* thou hast done, and thy thoughts *which are* to us-ward: they cannot be reckoned up in order unto thee: *if* I would declare and speak *of them*, **they are more than can be numbered**. *Psalm 40:5*

O God, **thou hast taught me from my youth**: and hitherto have I declared thy wondrous works. *Psalm 71:17*

Blessed *be* the LORD God, the God of Israel, who only doeth wondrous things. *Psalm 72:18*

Unto thee, O God, do we give thanks, *unto thee* do **we give thanks**: for *that* thy name is near thy wondrous works declare. *Psalm 75:1*

Thou *art* the God that doest wonders: **thou hast declared thy strength** among the people. *Psalm 77:14*

I will remember the works of the LORD: surely **I will remember thy wonders of old**. *Psalm 77:11*

Thou *art* the God that doest wonders: thou hast declared thy strength among the people. *Psalm 77:14*

For thou *art* great, and doest wondrous things: thou *art* God alone. *Psalm 86:10*

And the heavens shall praise thy wonders, O LORD: thy faithfulness also in the congregation of the saints. *Psalm 89:5*

Declare his glory among the heathen, his wonders among all people. *Psalm 96:3*

Sing unto him, sing psalms unto him: **talk ye of all his wondrous works**. *Psalm 105:2*

Remember his marvellous works that he hath done; his wonders, and the judgments of his mouth. *Psalm 105:5*

To him who alone doeth great wonders: for his mercy *endureth* for ever. *Psalm 136:4*

I will speak of the glorious honour of thy majesty, and of thy wondrous works. *Psalm 145:5*

O LORD, thou *art* my God; I will exalt thee, I will praise thy name; for **thou hast done wonderful *things*; *thy*** counsels of old *are* faithfulness *and* truth. *Isaiah 25:1*

How great *are* his signs! and **how mighty** *are* his wonders! his kingdom *is* an everlasting kingdom, and his dominion *is* from generation to generation. *Daniel 4:3*

Ye men of Israel, hear these words; Jesus of Nazareth, a man approved of God among you by miracles and wonders and signs, which **God did by him in the midst of you**, as ye yourselves also know. *Acts 2:22*

God also bearing *them* witness, both with **signs and wonders**, and with divers **miracles**, and gifts of the Holy Ghost, according to his own will? *Hebrews 2:4*

I PRAISE GOD BECAUSE HE...

Forgives

And the LORD passed by before him, and proclaimed, The LORD, The LORD God, merciful and gracious, longsuffering, and **abundant in goodness and truth**, Keeping mercy for thousands, forgiving iniquity and transgression and sin. *Exodus 34:6-7*

The LORD is **longsuffering**, and **of great mercy**, forgiving iniquity and transgression. *Numbers 14:18*

If my people, which are called by my name, shall humble themselves, and pray, and seek my face, and turn from their wicked ways; then will I hear from heaven, and will forgive their sin, and **will heal their land**. *II Chronicles 7:14*

I acknowledged my sin unto thee, and mine iniquity have I not hid. I **said, I will confess my transgressions unto the LORD; and thou** forgavest the iniquity of my sin. *Psalm 32:5*

For thou, Lord, *art* good, and **ready to forgive**; and **plenteous in mercy** unto all them that call upon thee. *Psalm 86:5*

If thou, LORD, shouldest mark iniquities, O Lord, who shall stand? But there is forgiveness with thee, **that thou mayest be feared**. *Psalm 130:3-4*

And they shall teach no more every man his neighbour, and every man his brother, saying, Know the LORD: for they shall all know me, from the least of them unto the greatest of them, saith the LORD: for I will forgive their iniquity, and **I will remember their sin no more**. *Jeremiah 31:34*

To the Lord our God *belong* **mercies and forgivenesses**, though we have rebelled against him. *Daniel 9:9*

Him hath God exalted with his right hand *to be* **a Prince and a Saviour**, for to give repentance to Israel, and forgiveness of sins. *Acts 5:31*

To open their eyes, *and* to turn *them* from darkness to light, and *from* the power of Satan unto God, that they may receive forgiveness of sins, and **inheritance among them which are sanctified by faith that is in me.** *Acts 26:18*

And be ye kind one to another, tenderhearted, forgiving one another, even as **God for Christ's sake hath forgiven you.** *Ephesians 4:32*

And you, being dead in your sins and the uncircumcision of your flesh, hath he quickened together with him, **having forgiven you all trespasses**. *Colossians 2:13*

And **the prayer of faith shall save the sick**, and the Lord shall raise him up; and if he have committed sins, they shall be forgiven him. *James 5:15*

If we confess our sins, he is **faithful and just** to forgive our sins, and to cleanse us from all unrighteousness. *I John 1:9*

I PRAISE GOD BECAUSE HE…

Gives

O God, *thou art* terrible out of thy holy places: the God of Israel *is* he that **giveth strength and power** unto *his* people. *Psalm 68:35*

For the LORD God is a sun and shield: the LORD will give **grace and glory**: no good thing will he withhold from them that walk uprightly. *Psalm 84:11*

For the LORD giveth **wisdom**: out of his mouth cometh knowledge and understanding. *Proverbs 2:6*

He giveth **power to the faint**; and to them that have no might he increaseth strength. *Isaiah 40:29*

If ye then, being evil, know how to give good gifts unto your children, how much more shall your Father which is in heaven give **good things** to them that ask him? *Matthew 7:11*

For God so loved the world, that he gave his only begotten Son, that whosoever believeth in him should not perish, but have everlasting life. *John 3:16*

And I will pray the Father, and he shall give you **another Comforter**, that he may abide with you for ever. *John 14:16*

God that made the world and all things therein, seeing that he is Lord of heaven and earth, dwelleth not in temples made with hands; Neither is worshipped with men's hands, as though he needed any thing, seeing he giveth to all **life, and breath**, and all things. *Acts 17:24-25*

And hope maketh not ashamed; because the love of God is shed abroad in our hearts by **the Holy Ghost** which is given unto us. *Romans 5:5*

He that spared not his own Son, but delivered him up for us all, how shall he not with him also **freely give us all things**? *Romans 8:32*

I thank my God always on your behalf, for **the grace of God** which is given you by Jesus Christ. *I Corinthians 1:4*

So then neither is he that planteth any thing, neither he that watereth; but God that **giveth the increase**. *I Corinthians 3:7*

But thanks *be* to God, which **giveth us the victory** through our Lord Jesus Christ. *1 Corinthians 15:57*

For God, who commanded the light to shine out of darkness, hath shined in our hearts, to *give* **the light of the knowledge of the glory of God** in the face of Jesus Christ. *II Corinthians 4:6*

Now he that hath wrought us for the selfsame thing *is* God, who also hath given unto us the **earnest of the Spirit**. *II Corinthians 5:5*

And all things *are* of God, who hath reconciled us to himself by Jesus Christ, and hath given to us **the ministry of reconciliation**. *II Corinthians 5:18*

Now our Lord Jesus Christ himself, and God, even our Father, which hath loved us, and hath given *us* **everlasting consolation and good hope through grace**. *II Thessalonians 2:16*

Charge them that are rich in this world, that they be not highminded, nor trust in uncertain riches, but in the living God, who **giveth us richly all things to enjoy**. *I Timothy 6:17*

For God hath not given us the spirit of fear; but of power, and of love, and of a sound mind. *II Timothy 1:7*

All scripture *is* given by inspiration of God, and *is* profitable for doctrine, for reproof, for correction, for instruction in righteousness. *II Timothy 3:16*

If any of you lack wisdom, let him ask of God, that **giveth to all** *men* **liberally**, and upbraideth not; and it shall be given him. *James 1:5*

But he giveth more grace. Wherefore he saith, God resisteth the proud, but **giveth grace** unto the humble. *James 4:6*

And this is the record, that God hath given to us eternal life, and **this life is in his Son.** *I John 5:11*

And we know that the Son of God is come, and hath given us **an understanding**, that we may know him that is true, and we are in him that is true, *even* in his Son Jesus Christ. This is the true God, and eternal life. *I John 5:20*

And there shall be no night there; and they need no candle, neither light of the sun; for **the Lord God giveth them light**: and they shall reign for ever and ever. *Revelation 22:5*

I PRAISE GOD BECAUSE HE...

Hears

And God **heard their groaning**, and God remembered his covenant with Abraham, with Isaac, and with Jacob. *Exodus 2:24*

If my people, which are called by my name, shall humble themselves, and pray, and seek my face, and turn from their wicked ways; **then will I hear from heaven**, and will forgive their sin, and will heal their land. *II Chronicles 7:14*

I cried unto the LORD with my voice, and **he heard me out of his holy hill**. *Psalm 3:4*

But know that the LORD hath set apart him that is godly for himself: **the LORD will hear when I call unto him.** *Psalm 4:3*

My voice shalt thou hear in the morning, O LORD; in the morning will I direct my prayer unto thee, and will look up. *Psalm 5:3*

The LORD hath heard my supplication; the LORD **will receive my prayer**. *Psalm 6:8-9*

LORD, thou hast **heard the desire of the humble**: thou wilt prepare their heart, thou wilt cause thine ear to hear. *Psalm 10:17*

In my distress I called upon the LORD, and cried unto my God: he heard my voice out of his temple, and **my cry came before him**, even into his ears. *Psalm 18:6*

For I said in my haste, I am cut off from before thine eyes: **nevertheless thou heardest the voice of my supplications** when I cried unto thee. *Psalm 31:22*

I sought the LORD, and he heard me, and **delivered me from all my fears**. This poor man cried, and the LORD heard him, and saved him out of all his troubles. *Psalm 34:4, 6*

I waited patiently for the LORD; and he inclined his ear unto me, and heard my cry. *Psalm 40:1*

Evening, and morning, and at noon, will I pray, and cry aloud: and he shall hear my voice. *Psalm 55:17*

For thou, O God, hast heard my vows: thou hast given me the heritage of those that fear thy name. *Psalm 61:5*

O thou that hearest prayer, **unto thee shall all flesh come**. *Psalm 65:2*

But verily God hath heard me; **he hath attended to the voice of my prayer**. *Psalm 66:19*

I love the LORD, because he hath heard my voice and my supplications. **Because he hath inclined his ear unto me**, therefore will I call upon him as long as I live. *Psalm 116:1-2*

I will praise thee: for thou hast heard me, and art become my salvation. *Psalm 118:21*

He will fulfil the desire of them that fear him: he also will hear their cry, and will save them.
Psalm 145:19

And it shall come to pass, that before they call, I will answer; and **while they are yet speaking**, I will hear. *Isaiah 65:24*

Therefore I will look unto the LORD; **I will wait for the God of my salvation**: my God will hear me. *Micah 7: 7*

They shall call upon my name, and **I will hear them**: I will say, It is my people: and they shall say, The LORD is my God. *Zechariah 13:9*

Now we know that God heareth not sinners: but if any man be a worshipper of God, and doeth his will, him he heareth. *John 9:31*

And this is the confidence that we have in him, that, **if we ask anything according to his will, he heareth us**; And we know that he heareth us, whatsoever we ask, we know that we have the petitions that we desired of him. *I John 5:14-15*

I PRAISE GOD BECAUSE HE...

Judges Righteously

Shall not **the Judge of all the earth** do right? *Genesis 18:25*

The adversaries of the LORD shall be broken to pieces; out of heaven shall he thunder upon them: **the LORD shall judge the ends of the earth**; and he shall give strength unto his king, and exalt the horn of his anointed. *I Samuel 2:10*

Then shall the trees of the wood sing out at the presence of the LORD, because **he cometh to judge the earth.** *I Chronicles 16:33*

And he shall **judge the world in righteousness**, he shall minister judgment to the people in uprightness. *Psalm 9:8*

The LORD is known by the judgment which he executeth: the wicked is snared in the work of his own hands. *Psalm 9:16*

The fear of the LORD is clean, enduring for ever: the judgments of the LORD are **true and righteous altogether.** *Psalm 19:9*

He loveth righteousness and judgment: the earth is full of the goodness of the LORD. *Psalm 33:5*

And the heavens shall declare his righteousness: for **God *is* judge himself.** *Psalm 50:6*

So that a man shall say, Verily *there is* **a reward for the righteous**: verily he is a God that judgeth in the earth. *Psalm 58:11*

O let the nations be glad and sing for joy: for thou shalt judge the people righteously, and govern the nations upon earth. *Psalm 67:4*

He *is* the LORD our God: **his judgments *are* in all the earth.** *Psalm 105:7*

The just LORD is in the midst thereof; **he will not do iniquity**: every morning doth he bring his judgment to light, he faileth not; but the unjust knoweth no shame. *Zephaniah 3:5*

Because **he hath appointed a day**, in the which he will judge the world in righteousness by that man whom he hath ordained; whereof he hath given assurance unto all men, in that he hath raised him from the dead. *Acts 17:31*

In the day when God **shall judge the secrets of men** by Jesus Christ according to my gospel. *Romans 2:16*

O the depth of the riches both of the wisdom and knowledge of God! **how unsearchable *are* his judgments**, and his ways past finding out! *Romans 11:33*

I charge *thee* therefore before God, and the Lord Jesus Christ, **who shall judge the quick and the dead** at his appearing and his kingdom. *II Timothy 4:1*

Henceforth there is laid up for me a crown of righteousness, which the Lord, **the righteous judge**, shall give me at that day: and not to me only, but unto all them also that love his appearing. *II Timothy 4:8*

To the general assembly and church of the firstborn, which are written in heaven, and to **God the Judge of all**, and to the spirits of just men made perfect. *Hebrews 12:23*

For the time *is come* that **judgment must begin at the house of God**: and if *it* first *begin* at us, what shall the end *be* of them that obey not the gospel of God? *I Peter 4:17*

Who shall **give account to him** that is ready to judge the quick and the dead. *I Peter 4:5*

And I heard another out of the altar say, Even so, Lord God Almighty, **true and righteous are thy judgments.** *Revelation 16: 7*

And I saw the dead, small and great, stand before God; and the books were opened: and another book was opened, which is *the book* of life:

and the dead were judged out of those things which were written in the books, according to their works. *Revelation 20:12*

I PRAISE GOD BECAUSE HE...

Knows

Talk no more so exceeding proudly; let not arrogancy come out of your mouth: for **the LORD is a God of knowledge**, and by him actions are weighed. *I Samuel 2:3*

Then hear thou in heaven thy dwelling place, and forgive, and do, and give to every man according to his ways, **whose heart thou knowest**; (for thou, even thou only, knowest the hearts of all the children of men). *I Kings 8:39*

But he **knoweth the way that I take**: when he hath tried me, I shall come forth as gold. *Job 23:10*

For the LORD **knoweth the way of the righteous**: but the way of the ungodly shall perish. *Psalm 1:6*

The LORD **knoweth the days of the upright**: and their inheritance shall be for ever. *Psalm 37:18*

I have preached righteousness in the great congregation: lo, I have not refrained my lips, O LORD, thou knowest. *Psalm 40:9*

Shall not God search this out? for **he knoweth the secrets of the heart**. *Psalm 44:21*

O God, **thou knowest my foolishness**; and my sins are not hid from thee. *Psalm 69:5*

For **he knoweth our frame**; he remembereth that we are dust. *Psalm 103:14*

Thou knowest my downsitting and mine uprising, **thou understandest my thought afar off**. For there is not a word in my tongue, but, lo, O LORD, thou knowest it altogether. *Psalm 139:2, 4*

But thou, O LORD, knowest me: **thou hast seen me, and tried mine heart** toward thee. *Jeremiah 12:3*

He revealeth the deep and secret things: **he knoweth what is in the darkness**, and the light dwelleth with him. *Daniel 2:22*

The LORD is good, a strong hold in the day of trouble; and **he knoweth them that trust in him**. *Nahum 1:7*

Be not ye therefore like unto them: for your Father knoweth what things ye have need of, **before ye ask him**. *Matthew 6:8*

But of that day and hour knoweth no man, no, not the angels of heaven, but **my Father only**. *Matthew 24:36*

For all these things do the nations of the world seek after: and **your Father knoweth that ye have need of these things**. *Luke 12:30*

And God, which **knoweth the hearts**, bare them witness, giving them the Holy Ghost, even as *he did* unto us. *Acts 15:8*

Nevertheless the foundation of God standeth sure, having this seal, The Lord **knoweth them that are his.** And, Let every one that nameth the name of Christ depart from iniquity. *II Timothy 2:19*

The Lord **knoweth how** to deliver the godly out of temptations, and to reserve the unjust unto the day of judgment to be punished: *II Peter 2:9*

For if our heart condemn us, **God is greater than our heart**, and knoweth all things. *I John 3:20*

I PRAISE GOD BECAUSE HE...

Leads, Guides, Directs

And the LORD went before them by day in a pillar of a cloud, **to lead them the way**; and by night in a pillar of fire, to give them light; to go by day and night. *Exodus 13:21*

Thou **in thy mercy hast led forth the people** which thou hast redeemed: th**ou hast guided them in thy strength** unto thy holy habitation. *Exodus 15:13*

Yet thou in thy manifold mercies forsookest them not in the wilderness: the pillar of the cloud departed not from them by day, to lead them in the way; neither the pillar of fire by night, to **shew them light, and the way wherein they should go**. *Nehemiah 9:19*

THE LORD is my shepherd; I shall not want. He maketh me to lie down in green pastures: he leadeth me beside the still waters. He restoreth my soul: **he leadeth me in the paths of righteousness for his name's sake**. *Psalm 23:1-3*

Lead me in thy truth, and teach me: for thou *art* the God of my salvation; on thee do I wait all the day. *Psalm 25:5*

The meek will he **guide in judgment**: and the meek will he teach his way. *Psalm 25:9*

I will instruct thee and teach thee **in the way which thou shalt go**: I will guide thee with mine eye. *Psalm 32:8*

For this God *is* our God for ever and ever: he will be our guide *even* **unto death**. *Psalm 48:14*

Nevertheless I *am* continually with thee: thou hast holden *me* by my right hand. **Thou shalt guide me with thy counsel**, and afterward receive me *to* glory. *Psalm 73:23-24*

Whither shall I go from thy spirit? or whither shall I flee from thy presence? If I ascend up into heaven, thou *art* there: if I make my bed in hell, behold, thou *art there. If* I take the wings of the morning, *and* dwell in the uttermost parts of the sea; **Even there shall thy hand lead me**, and thy right hand shall hold me. *Psalm 139:7-10*

Teach me to do thy will; for thou *art* my God: thy spirit *is* good; **lead me into the land of uprightness**. *Psalm 143:10*

Trust in the LORD with all thine heart; and lean not unto thine own understanding. In all thy ways acknowledge him, and **he shall direct thy paths**. *Proverbs 3:5-6*

Thus saith the LORD, thy Redeemer, the Holy One of Israel; I *am* the LORD thy God which teacheth thee to profit, **which leadeth thee by the way *that* thou shouldest go**. *Isaiah 48:17*

And the LORD **shall guide thee continually**, and satisfy thy soul in drought, and make fat thy bones: and thou shalt be like a watered garden, and like a spring of water, whose waters fail not. *Isaiah 58:11*

Where is he that brought them out of the sea with the shepherd of his flock? Where is he that put his holy spirit within him? That **led them by the right hand of Moses with his glorious arm**, dividing the water before them, to make himself an everlasting name? *Isaiah 63: 11-12*

To give light to them that sit in darkness and *in* the shadow of death, to **guide our feet into the way of peace**. *Luke 1:79*

To him the porter openeth; and the sheep hear his voice: **and he calleth his own sheep by name, and leadeth them** out. *John 10:3*

Howbeit when he, the Spirit of truth, is come, he will **guide you into all truth**: for he shall not speak of himself; but whatsoever he shall hear, *that* shall he speak: and he will show you things to come. *John 16:13*

Or despisest thou the riches of his goodness and forbearance and longsuffering; not knowing that the goodness of God **leadeth thee to repentance**? *Romans 2:4*

For the Lamb which is in the midst of the throne shall feed them, and **shall lead them unto living fountains of waters:** and God shall wipe away all tears from their eyes. *Revelation 7:17*

I PRAISE GOD BECAUSE HE

Loves, Cares

But because **the LORD loved you**, and because he would keep the oath which he had sworn unto your fathers, hath the LORD brought you out with a mighty hand, and redeemed you out of the house of bondmen, from the hand of Pharaoh king of Egypt. *Deuteronomy 7:8*

Nevertheless the LORD thy God would not hearken unto Balaam; but the LORD thy God turned the curse into a blessing unto thee, **because the LORD thy God loved thee**. *Deuteronomy 23:5*

The LORD openeth the eyes of the blind: the LORD raiseth them that are bowed down: **the LORD loveth the righteous**. *Psalm 146:8*

For **whom the LORD loveth he correcteth**; even as a father the son in whom he delighteth. *Proverbs 3:12*

In all their affliction he was afflicted, and the angel of his presence saved them: **in his love and in his pity** he redeemed them; and he bare them, and carried them all the days of old. *Isaiah 63:9*

Yea, I have loved thee **with an everlasting love**: therefore with lovingkindness have I drawn thee. *Jeremiah 31:3*

The LORD thy God in the midst of thee is mighty; he will save, he will rejoice over thee with joy; **he will rest in his love**, he will joy over thee with singing. *Zephaniah 3:17*

I have loved you, saith the LORD. *Malachi 1:2*

For God **so loved** the world, that he gave his only begotten Son, that whosoever believeth in him should not perish, but have everlasting life. *John 3:16*

Jesus answered and said unto him, If a man love me, he will keep my words: and my Father will love him, and **we will come unto him, and make our abode with him**. *John 14:23*

For **the Father himself loveth you**, because ye have loved me, and have believed that I came out from God. *John 16:27*

And I have declared unto them thy name, and will declare it: **that the love wherewith thou hast loved me may be in them**, and I in them. *John 17:26*

And hope maketh not ashamed; because the love of God is shed abroad in our hearts by the Holy Ghost which is given unto us. But **God commendeth his love toward us**, in that, while we were yet sinners, **Christ died for us**. *Romans 5:5, 8*

For I am persuaded, that neither death, nor life, nor angels, nor principalities, nor powers, nor things present, nor things to come, Nor height, nor depth, nor any other creature, shall be able to separate us from **the love of God, which is in Christ Jesus our Lord**. *Romans 8:38-39*

Finally, brethren, farewell. Be perfect, be of good comfort, be of one mind, live in peace; and the **God of love and peace shall be with you**. *II Corinthians 13:11*

But God, who is **rich in mercy**, for his great love wherewith he loved us, Even when we were dead in sins, hath quickened us together with Christ, (by grace ye are saved). *Ephesians 2:4-5*

Now our Lord Jesus Christ himself, and God, **even our Father, which hath loved us**, and hath given us everlasting consolation and good hope through grace, Comfort your hearts, and stablish you in every good word and work. *II Thessalonians 2:16-17*

But after that **the kindness and love of God our Saviour** toward man appeared. *Titus 3:4*

For **whom the Lord loveth he chasteneth**, and scourgeth every son whom he receiveth. *Hebrews 12:6*

Casting all your care upon him; for **he careth for you**. *I Peter 5:7*

Behold, **what manner of love** the Father hath bestowed upon us, that we should be called the sons of God: therefore the world knoweth us not, because it knew him not. *I John 3:1*

Beloved, let us love one another: for love is of God; and every one that loveth is born of God, and knoweth God. He that loveth not knoweth not God; for **God is love**. In this was manifested the love of God toward us, because that God sent his only begotten Son into the world, that we might live through him. Herein is love, not that we loved God, but that he loved us, and **sent his Son to be the propitiation for our sins**. *I John 4:7-10*

And we have known and believed the love that God hath to us. God is love; and **he that dwelleth in love dwelleth in God, and God in him**. *I John 4:16*

We love him, because **he first loved us**. If a man say, I love God, and hateth his brother, he is a liar: for he that loveth not his brother whom he hath seen, how can he love God whom he hath not seen? And this commandment have we from him, That he who loveth God love his brother also. *I John 4:19-21*

I PRAISE GOD BECAUSE HE...

Made Heaven & Earth

In the beginning God created the heaven and the earth. *Genesis 1: 1*

For in six days the LORD made heaven and earth, the sea, and all that in them is, and rested the seventh day: wherefore the LORD blessed the sabbath day, and hallowed it. *Exodus 20: 11*

For all **the gods of the people are idols**: but the LORD made the heavens. *I Chronicles 16:26*

Thou, even thou, art LORD alone; thou hast made heaven, the heaven of heavens, with all their hosts, the earth, and all things that are therein, the seas, and all that is therein, and thou preservest them all; and **the host of heaven worshippeth thee**. *Nehemiah 9:6*

By the word of the LORD were the heavens made; and all the host of them by the breath of his mouth. He gathereth the waters of the sea together as an heap: he layeth up the depth in storehouses. Let all the earth fear the LORD: let all the inhabitants of the world stand in awe of him. **For he spake, and it was done**; he commanded, and it stood fast. *Psalm 33:6-9*

Ye are blessed of the LORD which made heaven and earth. **The heaven, even the heavens, are the LORD'S**: but the earth hath he given to the children of men. *Psalm 115:15-16*

My help *cometh* **from the LORD**, which made heaven and earth. *Psalm 121:2*

To him that **by wisdom made the heavens**: for his mercy endureth for ever. To him that stretched out the earth above the waters: for his mercy endureth for ever. To him that made great lights: for his mercy endureth for ever: The sun to rule by day: for his mercy endureth for ever: The moon and stars to rule by night: for **his mercy endureth for ever**. *Psalm 136:5-9*

Praise ye the LORD. Praise ye the LORD from the heavens: praise him in the heights. Praise ye him, all his angels: praise ye him, all his hosts. Praise ye him, sun and moon: praise him, all ye stars of light. Praise him, ye heavens of heavens, and ye waters that be above the heavens. Let them praise the name of the LORD: for **he commanded, and they were created**. *Psalm 148:1-5*

Lift up your eyes on high, and behold who hath created these things, that bringeth out their host by number: **he calleth them all by names by the greatness of his might**, for that he is strong in power; not one faileth. *Isaiah 40:26*

Hast thou not known? hast thou not heard, *that* the everlasting God, the LORD, **the Creator of the ends of the earth**, fainteth not, neither is weary? *there is* no searching of his understanding. *Isaiah 40:28*

Thus saith God the LORD, he that created the heavens, and **stretched them out**; he that spread forth the earth, and that which cometh out of it; he that giveth breath unto the people upon it, and spirit to them that walk therein. *Isaiah 42:5*

He hath made the earth by his power, he hath established the world by his wisdom, and hath stretched out the heavens by his discretion. **When he uttereth his voice**, there is a multitude of waters in the heavens, and he causeth the vapours to ascend from the ends of the earth; he maketh lightnings with rain, and bringeth forth the wind out of his treasures. *Jeremiah 10:12-13*

Ah Lord GOD! behold, thou hast made the heaven and the earth by thy great power and stretched out arm, and **there is nothing too hard for thee**. *Jeremiah 32:17*

For, lo, he that formeth the mountains, and createth the wind, and declareth unto man what *is* his thought, that maketh the morning darkness, and treadeth upon the high places of the earth, **The LORD, The God of hosts, *is* his name**. *Amos 4:13*

And when they heard that, **they lifted up their voice to God with one accord**, and said, Lord, thou *art* God, which hast made heaven, and earth, and the sea, and all that in them is. *Acts 4:24*

God that made the world and all things therein, seeing that he is **Lord of heaven and earth**, dwelleth not in temples made with hands; Neither is worshipped with men's hands, as though he needed any thing, seeing he giveth to all life, and breath, and all things. *Acts 17:24-25*

And to make all *men* see what *is* the fellowship of the mystery, which from the beginning of the world hath been hid in God, **who created all things by Jesus Christ**. *Ephesians 3:9*

Thou art worthy, O Lord, to receive glory and honour and power: for thou hast created all things, and **for thy pleasure** they are and were created. *Revelation 4:11*

Saying with a loud voice, **Fear God**, and **give glory** to him; for the hour of his judgment is come: and **worship him** that made heaven, and earth, and the sea, and the fountains of waters. *Revelation 14:7*

I PRAISE GOD BECAUSE HE…

Preserves

For the LORD our God, he *it is* that brought us up and our fathers out of the land of Egypt, from the house of bondage, and which did those great signs in our sight, and **preserved us in all the way wherein we went**, and among all the people through whom we passed. *Joshua 24:17*

Thou, *even* thou, *art* LORD alone; thou hast made heaven, the heaven of heavens, with all their host, the earth, and all *things* that *are* therein, the seas, and all that *is* therein, and **thou preservest them all**; and the host of heaven worshippeth thee. *Nehemiah 9:6*

Thou shalt keep them, O LORD, thou shalt preserve them from this generation for ever. *Psalm 12:7*

O love the LORD, all ye his saints: for the LORD **preserveth the faithful**, and plentifully rewardeth the proud doer. *Psalm 31:23*

Thou art my hiding place; thou shalt **preserve me from trouble**; thou shalt compass me about with songs of deliverance. *Psalm 32:7*

For the LORD loveth judgment, and **forsaketh not his saints**; they are preserved for ever: but the seed of the wicked shall be cut off. *Psalm 37:28*

Withhold not thou thy tender mercies from me, O LORD: **let thy lovingkindness and thy truth continually preserve me.** *Psalm 40:11*

Ye that love the LORD, hate evil: he **preserveth the souls of his saints**; he delivereth them out of the hand of the wicked. *Psalm 97:10*

The LORD shall **preserve thee from all evil**: he shall preserve thy soul. The LORD shall preserve thy going out and thy coming in from this time forth, and even for evermore. *Psalm 121:7-8*

The LORD **preserveth all them that love him**: but all the wicked will he destroy. *Psalm 145:20*

He keepeth the paths of judgment, and **preserveth the way of his saints**. *Proverbs 2:8*

Thus saith the LORD, In an acceptable time have I heard thee, **and in a day of salvation have I helped thee: and I will preserve thee**, and give thee for a covenant of the people, to establish the earth, to cause to inherit the desolate heritages. *Isaiah 49:8*

And the very God of peace sanctify you wholly; and *I pray God* your whole spirit and soul and body be **preserved blameless** unto the coming of our Lord Jesus Christ. *I Thessalonians 5:23*

And the Lord shall deliver me from every evil work, and **will preserve me unto his heavenly kingdom**: to whom be glory for ever and ever. Amen. *II Timothy 4:18*

Jude, the servant of Jesus Christ, and brother of James, to them that are sanctified by God the Father, and **preserved in Jesus Christ**, *and* called. *Jude 1*

I PRAISE GOD BECAUSE HE…

Reigns

The LORD shall reign **for ever and ever**. *Exodus 15:18*

Let the heavens be glad, and let the earth rejoice: and let men say among the nations, The LORD reigneth. *I Chronicles 16:31*

Thine, O LORD, is the greatness, and the power, and the glory, and the victory, and the majesty: for all that is in the heaven and in the earth is thine; **thine is the kingdom**, O LORD, and thou art exalted as **head above all**. Both riches and honour come of thee, and **thou reignest over all**; and in thine hand is power and might; and in thine hand it is to make great, and to give strength unto all. *I Chronicles 29:11-12*

O LORD God of our fathers, art not thou God in heaven? and rulest not thou over all the kingdoms of the heathen? and **in thine hand is there not power and might**, so that none is able to withstand thee? *II Chronicles 20:6*

God reigneth over the heathen: God sitteth upon **the throne of his h**oliness. *Psalm 47:8*

He **ruleth by his power for ever**; his eyes behold the nations: let not the rebellious exalt themselves. *Psalm 66:7*

THE LORD reigneth, he is **clothed with majesty**; the LORD is clothed with strength, wherewith he hath girded himself: the world also is stablished, that it cannot be moved. Thy throne is established of old: thou art from everlasting. *Psalm 93:1-2*

Say among the heathen that **the LORD reigneth**: the world also shall be established that it shall not be moved: he shall judge the people righteously. *Psalm 96:10*

THE LORD reigneth; **let the earth rejoice**; let the multitude of isles be glad thereof. Clouds and darkness are round about him: righteousness and judgment are the habitation of his throne. *Psalm 97:1-2*

THE LORD reigneth; let the people tremble: **he sitteth between the cherubims**; let the earth be moved. *Psalm 99:1*

The LORD hath **prepared his throne in the heavens**; and his kingdom ruleth over all. *Psalm 103:19*

The LORD sha**ll reign for ever**, even thy God, O Zion, unto all generations. Praise ye the LORD. *Psalm 146:10*

How beautiful upon the mountains are the feet of him that bringeth good tidings, that publisheth peace; that bringeth good tidings of good, that publisheth salvation; that saith unto Zion, **Thy God reigneth**! *Isaiah 52:7*

I blessed the most High, and I praised and honoured him that liveth for ever, **whose dominion is an everlasting dominion**, and his kingdom is from generation to generation. *Daniel 4:34*

And the seventh angel sounded; and there were great voices in heaven, saying, The kingdoms of this world are become the kingdoms of our Lord, and of his Christ; and he shall reign for ever and ever. ...We give thee thanks, O Lord God Almighty, which art, and wast, and art to come; because **thou hast taken to thee thy great power**, and hast reigned. *Revelation 11:15, 17*

And I heard as it were the voice of a great multitude, and as the voice of many waters, and as the voice of mighty thunderings, saying, **Alleluia: for the Lord God omnipotent reigneth**. *Revelation 19:6*

I PRAISE GOD BECAUSE HE...

Saves, Redeems

For the LORD your God *is* he that goeth with you, to **fight for you against your enemies**, to save you. *Deuteronomy 20:4*

The God of my rock; in him will I trust: *he is* my shield, and the horn of my salvation, my high tower, and **my refuge**, my saviour; thou savest me from violence. *II Samuel 22:3*

My defence *is* of God, which **saveth the upright in heart**. *Psalm 7:10*

This poor man cried, and the LORD heard *him*, and **saved him out of all his troubles**. *Psalm 34:6*

The LORD *is* nigh unto them that are of a broken heart; and **saveth such as be of a contrite spirit**. *Psalm 34:18*

And the LORD shall help them, and deliver them: he shall deliver them from the wicked, and save them, **because they trust in him**. *Psalm 37:40*

As for me, **I will call upon God**; and the LORD shall save me. *Psalm 55:16*

My lips shall greatly rejoice when I sing unto thee; and **my soul, which thou hast redeemed**. *Psalm 71:23*

Turn us again, O LORD God of hosts, **cause thy face to shine**; and we shall be saved. *Psalm 80:19*

Save us, O LORD our God, and gather us from among the heathen, to give thanks unto thy holy name, *and* to **triumph in thy praise**. *Psalm 106:47*

Then they cry unto the LORD in their trouble, *and* he **saveth them out of their distresses**. *Psalm 107:19*

Help me, O LORD my God: O **save me according to thy mercy**. *Psalm 109:26*

Though I walk in the midst of trouble, thou wilt revive me: thou shalt stretch forth thine hand against the wrath of mine enemies, and **thy right hand shall save me**. *Psalm 138:7*

He will fulfill the desire of them that fear him: **he also will hear their cry**, and will save them. *Psalm 145:19*

Say not thou, I will recompense evil; but **wait on the LORD**, and he shall save thee. *Proverbs 20:22*

And it shall be said in that day, Lo, this is our God; we have waited for him, and he will save us: this is the LORD; we have waited for him, **we will be glad and rejoice in his salvation**. *Isaiah 25:9*

For the LORD *is* our judge, the LORD *is* our lawgiver, the LORD *is* our king**; he will save us**. *Isaiah 33:22*

Say to them *that are* of a fearful heart, Be strong, fear not: behold, your God will come *with* vengeance, *even* God *with* a recompense; **he will come and save you**. *Isaiah 35:4*

Now therefore, O LORD our God, save us from his hand, **that all the kingdoms of the earth may know that thou *art* the LORD**, *even* thou only. *Isaiah 37:20*

Is my hand shortened at all, that it cannot redeem? or have I no power to deliver? behold, at my rebuke I dry up the sea, I make the rivers a wilderness. *Isaiah 50:2*

O Lord, thou hast pleaded the causes of my soul; **thou hast redeemed my life**. *Lamentations 3:58*

The LORD thy God in the midst of thee is mighty; he will save, **he will rejoice over thee with joy**; he will rest in his love, he will joy over thee with singing. *Zephaniah 3:17*

For God so loved the world, that he gave his only begotten Son, that whosoever believeth in him should not perish, but have everlasting life.

For God sent not his Son into the world to condemn the world; but **that the world through him might be saved.** *John 3:16-17*

For if, when we were enemies, we were reconciled to God by the death of his Son, **much more, being reconciled, we shall be saved by his life.** *Romans 5:10*

That if thou shalt **confess with thy mouth the Lord Jesus**, and shalt **believe in thine heart that God hath raised him from the dead**, thou shalt be saved. *Romans 10:9*

But when the fulness of the time was come, God sent forth his Son, made of a woman, made under the law, **to redeem them that were under the law**, that we might receive the adoption of sons. *Galatians 4:4-5*

For by grace are ye **saved through faith**; and that not of yourselves: *it is* the gift of God. *Ephesians 2:8*

Who hath saved us, and called us with an holy calling, **not according to our works**, but according to his own purpose and grace, which was given us in Christ Jesus before the world began. *II Timothy 1:9*

But after that the kindness and love of God our Saviour toward man appeared, Not by works of righteousness which we have done, but **according to his mercy he saved us**, by the washing of regeneration, and renewing of the Holy Ghost. *Titus 3:4-5*

Wherefore he is **able also to save them to the uttermost** that come unto God by him, seeing he ever liveth to make intercession for them. *Hebrews 7:25*

I PRAISE GOD BECAUSE HE…

Teaches

Good and upright is the LORD: therefore will he teach sinners in the way. The meek will he guide in judgment: and **the meek will he teach his way.** What man is he that feareth the LORD? him shall he teach in the way that he shall choose. *Psalm 25:8-9, 12*

I will instruct thee and teach thee in **the way which thou shalt go**: I will guide thee with mine eye. *Psalm 32:8*

O God, **thou hast taught me from my youth**: and hitherto have I declared thy wondrous works. *Psalm 71:17*

Blessed is the man whom thou chastenest, O LORD, and teachest him out of thy law. *Psalm 94:12*

I have not departed from thy judgments: for thou hast taught me. *Psalm 119:102*

My lips shall utter praise, when **thou hast taught me thy statutes**. *Psalm 119:171*

And many people shall go and say, Come ye, and let us go up to the mountain of the LORD, to the house of the God of Jacob; and he will teach us of his ways, and **we will walk in his paths**: for out of Zion shall go forth the law, and the word of the LORD from Jerusalem. *Isaiah 2:3*

Thus saith the LORD, thy Redeemer, the Holy One of Israel; I *am* the LORD thy God **which teacheth thee to profit**, which leadeth thee by the way *that* thou shouldest go. *Isaiah 48:17*

And **all thy children shall be taught of the LORD**; and great shall be the peace of thy children. *Isaiah 54:13*

And many nations shall come, and say, Come, and let us go up to the mountain of the LORD, and to the house of the God of Jacob; **and he will teach us of his ways**, and we will walk in his paths: for the law shall go forth of Zion, and the word of the LORD from Jerusalem. *Micah 4:2*

All scripture is given by inspiration of God, and is profitable for doctrine, for reproof, for correction, for **instruction in righteousness.** *II Timothy 3:16*

Divine Names & Titles

DIVINE NAMES & TITLES

Abba. *Romans 8:15*
Advocate. *I John 2:1*
Almighty. *Genesis 17:1; Matthew 28:18; Revelation 1:8*
Alpha and Omega. *Revelation 1:8; 22:13*
Amen. *Revelation 3:14*
Ancient of Days. *Daniel 7:9*
Anointed One. *Psalm 2:2*
Apostle of our Profession. *Hebrews 3:1*
Atoning Sacrifice for our sins. *I John 2:2*
Author and Perfecter of our faith. *Hebrews 12:2*
Author of Life. *Acts 3:15*
Author of Salvation. *Hebrews 2:10*

Beginning. *Revelation 21:6*
Beginning and End. *Revelation 22:13*
Blessed and only Ruler. *I Timothy 6:15*
Bread of God. *John 6:33*
Bread of Life. *John 6:35; 6:48*
Bridegroom. *Matthew 9:15*
Branch. *Jeremiah 33:15*
Bridegroom. *Isaiah 62:56*
Bright Morning Star. *Revelation 22:16*

Chief Cornerstone. *Ephesians 2:20*
Chief Shepherd. *I Peter 5:4*
Chosen One. *Isaiah 42:1*
Christ. *I John 2:22*
Christ of God. *Luke 9:2*
Christ the Lord. *Luke 2:11*
Comforter. *John 14:26*
Consolation of Israel. *Luke 2:25*
Consuming Fire. *Hebrews 12:29*
Counselor. *Isaiah 9:6*
Creator. *John 1:3*

Deliverer. Romans 11:26
Door. *John 10:7*

End. *Revelation 21:6*

Eternal God. *Deuteronomy 33:27*
Eternal Life. *I John 1:2*
Everlasting Father. *Isaiah 9:6*

Faithful and True. *Revelation 19:11*
Faithful and True Witness. *Revelation 3:14*
Father. *Matthew 6:9*
First and Last. *Revelation 1:17; 22:13*
Firstborn from the dead. *Revelation 1:5*
Firstborn over all creation. *Colossians 1:15*
Firstfruits. *I Corinthians 15:20-23*
Foundation. *I Corinthians 3:11*
Friend of tax collectors and sinners. *Matthew 11:19*

Gate. *John 10:9*
God. *Genesis 1:1; John 1:1*
God Over All. *Romans 9:5*
God Who Sees Me. *Genesis 16:13*
Good Shepherd. *John 10:11,14*
Great Shepherd. *Hebrews 13:20*
Great High Priest. *Hebrews 4:14*
Guide. *Psalm 48:14*

Head of the Body. *Colossians 1:18*
Head of the Church. *Ephesians 1:22*
Heir of all things. *Hebrews 1:2*
High Priest. *Hebrews 2:17*
Holy and True. *Revelation 3:7*
Holy One. *Acts 3:14*
Holy One of Israel. *Isaiah 49:7*
Holy Spirit. *John 16:26*
Hope. *I Timothy 1:1*
Hope of Glory. *Colossians 1:27*
Horn of Salvation. *Luke 1:69*

I Am. *John 8:58*
Image of God. *II Corinthians 4:4*
Image of His Person. *Hebrews 1:3*
Immanuel. *Matthew 1:23*

Jesus. *Matthew 1:21*

Jesus Christ Our Lord. *Romans 6:23*
Judge of the living and the dead. *Acts 10:42*

King. *Zechariah 9:9*
King Eternal. *I Timothy 1:17*
King of Israel. *John 1:49*
King of Kings. *I Timothy 6:15*
King of the Ages. *Revelation 15:3*
King of the Jews. *Matthew. 27:11*

Lamb. *Revelation 13:8*
Lamb of God. *John 1:29*
Lamb Without Blemish. *I Peter 1:19*
Last Adam. *I Corinthians 15:45*
Lawgiver. *Isaiah 33:22*
Life. *Colossians 3:4*
Light of the World. *John 8:12*
Lion of the Tribe of Judah. *Revelation 5:5*
Living One. *Revelation 1:18*
Living Stone. *II Peter 2:4*
Living Water. *John 4:10*
Lord. *II Peter 2:20*
Lord God Almighty. *Revelation 15:3*
Lord of All. *Acts 10:36*
Lord of Glory. *I Corinthians 2:8*
Lord of Lords. *Revelation 19:16*
Lord Our Righteousness. *Jeremiah 23:6*
Love. *I John 4:8*

Man of Sorrows. *Isaiah 53:3*
Master. *Luke 9:33*
Mediator of the New Covenant. *Hebrews 9:15*
Merciful God. *Jeremiah 3:12*
Messiah. *John 4:25*
Mighty God. *Isaiah 9:6*
Mighty One. *Isaiah 60:16*
Morning Star. *Revelation 22:16*

Offspring of David. *Revelation 22:16*
Omega. *Revelation 22:13*

One Mediator. *I Timothy 2:5*
Only Begotten Son of God. *John 1:18; I John 4:9*
Our Great God and Savior. *Titus 2:13*
Our Holiness. *I Corinthians 1:30*
Our Husband. *II Corinthians 11:2*
Our Protection. *II Thessalonians. 3:3*
Our Redemption. *I Corinthians 1:30*
Our Righteousness. *I Corinthians 1:30*
Our Sacrificed Passover Lamb. *I Corinthians 5:7*

Passover Lamb. *I Corinthians 5:7*
Potter. *Isaiah 64:8*
Power of God. *I Corinthians 1:24*
Precious Cornerstone. *I Peter 2:6*
Prophet. *Acts 3:22*
Prince of Peace. *Isaiah 9:6*
Purifier. *Malachi 3:3*

Rabbi. Matthew 26:25
Radiance of God's Glory. *Hebrews 1:3*
Redeemer. *Job 19:25*
Resurrection and Life. John 11:25
Righteous Branch. *Jeremiah 23:5*
Righteous One. *Acts 7:52*
Rock. *I Corinthians 10:4*
Root of David. *Revelation 5:5; 22:16*
Ruler of God's Creation. *Revelation 3:14*
Ruler of the Kings of the Earth. *Revelation 1:5*
Ruler over Israel. *Micah 5:2*

Savior. *Ephesians 5:23*
Scepter out of Israel. *Numbers 24:17*
Seed. *Genesis 3:15*
Servant. *Isaiah 42:1*
Shepherd of Our Souls. *1 Peter 2:25*
Shield. *Genesis 15:1*
Son of David. *Luke 18:39*
Son of God. *John 1:49; Hebrews 4:14*
Son of Man. *Matthew 8:20*
Son of the Most High God. *Luke 1:32*
Source of Eternal Salvation. *Hebrews 5:9*

Spirit of God. *Genesis 1:2*
Star out of Jacob. *Numbers 24:17*
Stone the builders rejected. *Acts 4:11*
Sun of Righteousness. *Malachi 4:2*

Teacher. *John 13:13*
True Bread. *John 6:32*
True Light. *John 1:9*
True Vine. *John 15:1*
Truth. *John 1:14; 14:6*
True Witness. *Revelation 3:14*

Way. *John 14:6*
Wisdom of God. *1 Corinthians 1:24*
Wonderful Counselor. *Isaiah 9:6*
Word. *John 1:1*
Word of God. *Revelation 19:13*

PRINCIPAL OLD TESTAMENT NAMES FOR GOD

Yah'weh "I am [the Eternal One, the Uncreated One, I will be]." *Genesis 2:4*

Adonai "Lord." *Malachi 1:6*

Elohim "God [Plural form implying majesty and plurality in unity]" *Genesis 1:1*

El 'Elyon "The most high God." *Genesis 14:19*

El Ro'I "The God who sees." *Genesis 16:13*

El Shaddai "God Almighty." *Genesis 17:1*

El 'Olam "The everlasting God." *Isaiah 40:28*

Adonai Rohi "The Lord my shepherd." *Psalm 23:1*

Adonai Shamah "The Lord who is present." *Ezekiel 48:35*

Adonai Rapha "The Lord our healer." *Exodus 15:26*

Adonai Tzidkenu "The Lord our righteousness." *Jeremiah 23:6*

Adonai 'Yir'eh "The Lord will provide." *Genesis 22:13'14*

Adonai Nissi "The Lord my banner, my victory." *Exodus 17:15*

Adonai Shalom "The Lord is peace." *Judges 6:24*

Adonai Tzva'ot "The Lord of Hosts [of the Armies of Heaven]." *Isaiah 6:13*

Worshiping Jesus

WORSHIPING JESUS

For unto us a child is born, unto us a son is given: and the government shall be upon his shoulder: and his name shall be called **Wonderful, Counsellor, The mighty God, The everlasting Father, The Prince of Peace.** *Isaiah 9:6*

Saying, Where is he that is born **King of the Jews**? for we have seen his star in the east, and are come to worship him. *Matthew 2:2*

And when they were come into the house, they saw the young child with Mary his mother, and fell down, and worshipped him: and when they had opened their treasures, **they presented unto him gifts**; gold, and frankincense, and myrrh. *Matthew 2:11*

And, behold, there came a leper and worshipped him, saying, Lord, **if thou wilt**, thou canst make me clean. *Matthew 8:2*

While he spake these things unto them, behold, there came a certain ruler, and worshipped him, saying, My daughter is even now dead: but come and lay thy hand upon her, and **she shall live**. *Matthew 9:18*

Then they that were in the ship came and worshipped him, saying, Of a truth **thou art the Son of God**. *Matthew 14:33*

And, behold, a woman of Canaan came out of the same coasts, and cried unto him, saying, Have mercy on me, O Lord, *thou* Son of David; my daughter is grievously vexed with a devil. But he answered her not a word. And his disciples came and besought him, saying, Send her away; for she crieth after us. But he answered and said, I am not sent but unto the lost sheep of the house of Israel. Then came she and worshipped him, saying, **Lord, help me.** *Matthew 15:22-25*

Then came to him the mother of Zebedee's children with her sons, worshipping *him*, and **desiring a certain thing of him**. *Matthew 20:20*

And as they went to tell his disciples, behold, Jesus met them, saying, All hail. **And they came and held him by the feet**, and worshipped him. *Matthew 28:9*

And when they saw him, they worshipped him: but **some doubted**. *Matthew 28:17*

But when he saw Jesus afar off, **he ran** and worshipped him. *Mark 5:6*

And they worshipped him, and returned to Jerusalem with **great joy**. *Luke 24:52*

And he said, **Lord, I believe**. And he worshipped him. *John 9:38*

Looking for that **blessed hope**, and the glorious appearing of the great God and our Saviour Jesus Christ. *Titus 2:13*

And again, when he bringeth in the firstbegotten into the world, he saith, And **let all the angels of God worship him**. *Hebrews 1:6*

Seeing then that we have a **great high priest**, that is passed into the heavens, Jesus the Son of God, let us hold fast *our* profession. *Hebrews 4:14*

Now the God of peace, that brought again from the dead our Lord Jesus, that **great shepherd of the sheep**, through the blood of the everlasting covenant. *Hebrews 13:20*

And I turned to see the voice that spake with me. And being turned, I saw seven golden candlesticks; And in the midst of the seven candlesticks *one* like unto the Son of man, clothed with a garment down to the foot, and girt about the paps with a golden girdle. **His head and *his* hairs *were* white like wool, as white as snow**; and **his eyes *were* as a flame of fire**; And **his feet like unto fine brass**, as if they burned in a furnace; and **his voice as the sound of many waters**. And he had in his right hand seven stars: and out of his mouth went a sharp two-edged sword: and his countenance *was* as the sun shineth in his strength. And when I saw him, **I fell at his feet as dead**. *Revelation 1:12-17*

And they sung a new song, saying,
Thou art worthy to take the book, and to open the seals thereof: for **thou wast slain, and hast redeemed us to God by thy blood** out of every kindred, and tongue, and people, and nation; [10]And hast made us unto our God kings and priests: and we shall reign on the earth. [11]And I beheld, and I heard the voice of many angels round about the throne and

the beasts and the elders: and the number of them was ten thousand times ten thousand, and thousands of thousands;
Saying with a loud voice,
Worthy is the Lamb that was slain to receive **power, and riches, and wisdom, and strength, and honour, and glory, and blessing**. And every creature which is in heaven, and on the earth, and under the earth, and such as are in the sea, and all that are in them, heard I saying, Blessing, and honour, and glory, and power, *be* unto him that sitteth upon the throne, and unto the Lamb for ever and ever. And the four beasts said, Amen. And the four *and* twenty elders fell down and worshipped him **that liveth for ever and ever**. *Revelation 5:9-14*

I Praise Jesus Because He is…

I PRAISE JESUS BECAUSE HE IS…

King

Rejoice greatly, O daughter of Zion; shout, o daughter of Jerusalem: behold, thy King cometh unto thee: **he is just, and having salvation; lowly**, and riding upon an ass, and upon a colt the foal of an ass. *Zechariah 9:9*

Saying, Where is he that is **born King of the Jews**? for we have seen his star in the east, and are come to worship him. *Matthew 2:2*

And set up over his head his accusation written, THIS IS **JESUS THE KING OF THE JEWS**. *Matthew 27:37*

And when he was come nigh, even now at the descent of the mount of Olives, the whole multitude of the disciples began to rejoice and praise God with a loud voice for all the mighty works that they had seen; Saying, **Blessed be the King** that cometh in the name of the Lord: peace in heaven, and glory in the highest. *Luke 19:37-38*

On the next day much people that were come to the feast, when they heard that Jesus was coming to Jerusalem, Took branches of palm trees, and went forth to meet him, and cried, Hosanna: **Blessed is the King of Israel** that cometh in the name of the Lord. *John 12:12-13*

Pilate therefore said unto him, Art thou a king then? Jesus answered, Thou sayest that I am a king. **To this end was I born**, and for this cause came I into the world, that I should bear witness unto the truth. Every one that is of the truth heareth my voice. *John 18:37*

These shall make war with the Lamb, and the Lamb shall overcome them: for he **is Lord of lords, and King of kings**: and they that are with him are called, and chosen, and faithful. *Revelation 17:14*

And he hath on his vesture and on his thigh **a name written, KING OF KINGS, AND LORD OF LORDS**. *Revelation 19:16*

I PRAISE JESUS BECAUSE HE IS...

The Lamb of God

He was oppressed, and he was afflicted, yet he opened not his mouth: he is brought **as a lamb to the slaughter**, and as a sheep before her shearers is dumb, so he openeth not his mouth. *Isaiah 53:7*

The next day John seeth Jesus coming unto him, and saith, Behold the Lamb of God, **which taketh away the sin of the world.** *John 1:29*

Forasmuch as ye know that ye were not redeemed with corruptible things, as silver and gold, from your vain conversation received by tradition from your fathers; But with the **precious blood** of Christ, **as of a lamb without blemish and without spot.** *I Peter 1:18-19*

And I beheld, and, lo, in the midst of the throne and of the four beasts, and in the midst of the elders, stood **a Lamb as it had been slain**, having seven horns and seven eyes, which are the seven Spirits of God sent forth into all the earth. *Revelation 5:6*

And when he had taken the book, the four beasts and four and twenty elders **fell down before the Lamb**, having every one of them harps, and golden vials full of odours, which are the prayers of saints. And they sung a new song, saying, **Thou art worthy** to take the book, and to open the seals thereof: for thou wast slain, and hast redeemed us to God by thy blood out of every kindred, and tongue, and people, and nation. *Revelation 5:8-9*

Worthy is the Lamb that was slain to receive power, and riches, and wisdom, and strength, and honour, and glory, and blessing. And every creature which is in heaven, and on the earth, and under the earth, and such as are in the sea, and all that are in them, heard I saying, Blessing, and honour, and glory, and power, be unto him that sitteth upon the throne, and unto the Lamb **for ever and ever.** *Revelation 5:12-13*

After this I beheld, and, lo, a great multitude, which no man could number, of all nations, and kindreds, and people, and tongues, stood before the throne, and before the Lamb, clothed with white robes, and palms in their hands; And cried with a loud voice, saying, **Salvation to**

our God which sitteth upon the throne, and unto the Lamb. *Revelation 7:9-10*

And he said to me, These are they which came out of great tribulation, and have washed their robes, and **made them white in the blood of the Lamb**. They shall hunger no more, neither thirst any more; neither shall the sun light on them, nor any heat. For the Lamb which is in the midst of the throne shall feed them, and shall lead them unto living fountains of waters: and God shall wipe away all tears from their eyes. *Revelation 7:14, 16-17*

And they overcame him by the blood of the Lamb, and by the word of their testimony; and they loved not their lives unto the death. *Revelation 12:11*

And they sing the song of Moses the servant of God, and **the song of the Lamb**, saying, Great and marvellous *are* thy works, Lord God Almighty; just and true *are* thy ways, thou King of saints. *Revelation 15:3*

Let us be glad and rejoice, and give honour to him: for **the marriage of the Lamb** is come, and **his wife hath made herself ready**. And to her was granted that she should be arrayed in fine linen, clean and white: for the fine linen is the righteousness of saints. And he saith unto me, Write, Blessed are they which are called unto the marriage supper of the Lamb. And he saith unto me, These are the true sayings of God. *Revelation 19:7-9*

And he showed me **a pure river of water of life**, clear as crystal, proceeding out of the throne of God and of the Lamb. *Revelation 22:1*

And I saw no temple therein: for the Lord God Almighty and the Lamb are the temple of it. And the city had no need of the sun, neither of the moon, to shine in it: for the glory of God did lighten it, and **the Lamb is the light thereof**. *Revelation 21:22-23*

And there shall be **no more curse**: but the throne of God and of the Lamb shall be in it; and his servants shall serve him. *Revelation 22:3*

I PRAISE JESUS BECAUSE HE IS...

Light

And after six days Jesus taketh Peter, James, and John his brother, and bringeth them up into an high mountain apart, And was transfigured before them: and **his face did shine as the sun**, and his raiment was white as the light. *Matthew 17:1-2*

For mine eyes have seen thy salvation, Which thou hast prepared before the face of all people; **A light to lighten the Gentiles**, and the glory of thy people Israel. *Luke 2:30-32*

In him was life; and **the life was the light of men**. And the light shineth in darkness; and the darkness comprehended it not. There was a man sent from God, whose name was John. The same came for a witness, to **bear witness of the Light**, that all men through him might believe. He was not that Light, but was sent to bear witness of that Light. That was **the true Light**, which lighteth every man that cometh into the world. *John 1:4-9*

And this is the condemnation, that **light is come into the world**, and men loved darkness rather than light, because their deeds were evil. *John 3:19*

Then spake Jesus again unto them, saying, I am **the light of the world**: he that followeth me shall not walk in darkness, but shall have **the light of life**. *John 8:12*

As long as I am in the world, I am the light of the world. *John 9:5*

Then Jesus said unto them, Yet a little while is the light with you. Walk while ye have the light, lest darkness come upon you: for he that walketh in darkness knoweth not whither he goeth. While ye have light, **believe in the light**, that ye may be the children of light. *John 12:35-36*

I am come a light into the world, that whosoever believeth on me should not abide in darkness. *John 12:46*

For God, who commanded the light to shine out of darkness, hath shined in our hearts, to give **the light of the know ledge of the glory of God in the face of Jesus Christ**. *II Corinthians 4:6*

But **if we walk in the light**, as he is in the light, we have fellowship one with another, and the blood of Jesus Christ his Son cleanseth us from all sin. *I John 1:7*

I PRAISE JESUS BECAUSE HE IS…

Lord

And they feared exceedingly, and said one to another, What manner of man is this, that even **the wind and the sea obey him**? *Mark 4:41*

For unto you is born this day in the city of David a Saviour, which is **Christ the Lord**. *Luke 2:11*

The Son of man is **Lord also of the sabbath**. *Luke 6:5*

So when they had rowed about five and twenty or thirty furlongs, they see Jesus **walking on the sea**, and drawing nigh unto the ship: and they were afraid. *John 6:19*

Ye call me **Master and Lord**: and ye say well; for so I am. *John 13:13*

And Thomas answered and said unto him, **My Lord and my God**. *John 20:28*

Therefore let all the house of Israel know assuredly, that God hath made that same Jesus, **whom ye have crucified**, both Lord and Christ. *Acts 2:36*

The word which *God* sent unto the children of Israel, **preaching peace** by Jesus Christ: (he is Lord of all) *Acts 10:36*

For the wages of sin *is* death; but the gift of God *is* **eternal life through Jesus Christ our Lord**. *Romans 6:23*

Nor height, nor depth, nor any other creature, shall be able to separate us from **the love of God, which is in Christ Jesus our Lord**. *Romans 8:39*

For to this end Christ both died, and rose, and revived, that he might be **Lord both of the dead and living**. *Romans 14:9*

Unto the church of God which is at Corinth, to them that are sanctified in Christ Jesus, called *to be* saints, with all that in every place **call upon the**

name of Jesus Christ our Lord, both theirs and ours. *I Corinthians 1:2*

God *is* faithful, by whom ye were called unto **the fellowship of his Son Jesus Christ our Lord.** *I Corinthians 1:9*

Blessed *be* the God and Father of our Lord Jesus Christ, who hath **blessed us with all spiritual blessings in heavenly** *places* **in Christ**. *Ephesians 1:3*

Giving thanks always for all things unto God and the Father in the name of our Lord Jesus Christ. *Ephesians 5:20*

And *that* every tongue should **confess that Jesus Christ** *is* **Lord**, to the glory of God the Father. *Philippians 2:11*

Let the word of Christ dwell in you richly in all wisdom; teaching and admonishing one another in psalms and hymns and spiritual songs, **singing with grace in your hearts to the Lord.** *Colossians 3:16*

That the **name of our Lord Jesus Christ may be glorified in you**, and ye in him, according to the grace of our God and the Lord Jesus Christ. *II Thessalonians 1:12*

I PRAISE JESUS BECAUSE HE IS

Our Savior

And the angel said unto them, Fear not: for, behold, I bring you good tidings of great joy, which shall be to all people. For unto you is born this day in the city of David a Saviour, which is **Christ the Lord**. *Luke 2:10-11*

Now we believe, not because of thy saying: for we have heard him ourselves, and know that this is indeed the Christ, the **Saviour of the world**. *John 4:42*

Him hath God exalted with his right hand to be **a Prince and a Saviour**, for to give repentance to Israel, and forgiveness of sins. *Acts 5:31*

For the husband is the head of the wife, even as Christ is the head of the church: and he is **the saviour of the body**. *Ephesians 5:23*

For our conversation is in heaven; from whence also **we look for the Saviour**, the Lord Jesus Christ. *Philippians 3:20*

Paul, an apostle of Jesus Christ by the commandment of God our Saviour, and Lord Jesus Christ, *which is* **our hope**. *I Timothy 1:1*

But is now made manifest by the appearing of our Saviour Jesus Christ, who hath abolished death, and **hath brought life and immortality to light through the gospel**. *II Timothy 1:10*

To Titus, *mine* own son after the common faith: **Grace, mercy,** *and* **peace**, from God the Father and the Lord Jesus Christ our Saviour. *Titus 1:4*

Looking for that **blessed hope**, and **the glorious appearing** of the great God and our Saviour Jesus Christ. *Titus 2:13*

Simon Peter, a servant and an apostle of Jesus Christ, to them that have obtained like **precious faith** with us through the righteousness of God and our Saviour Jesus Christ. *II Peter 1:1*

For so an entrance shall be ministered unto you abundantly into **the everlasting kingdom** of our Lord and Saviour Jesus Christ. *II Peter 1:11*

For if after they have escaped the pollutions of the world **through the knowledge** of the Lord and Saviour Jesus Christ, they are again entangled therein, and overcome, the latter end is worse with them than the beginning. *II Peter 2:20*

But **grow in grace, and** *in* **the knowledge** of our Lord and Saviour Jesus Christ. To him *be* glory both now and for ever. Amen. *II Peter 3:18*

And we have seen and do testify that the **Father sent the Son** *to be* the Saviour of the world. *I John 4:14*

I PRAISE JESUS BECAUSE HE IS…

The Son of God

Thy throne, O God, is for ever and ever: the sceptre of thy kingdom is a right sceptre. Thou lovest righteousness, and hatest wickedness: therefore God, thy God, hath anointed thee with the oil of gladness above thy fellows. *Psalm 45:6-7*

For unto us a child is born, unto us a son is given: and the government shall be upon his shoulder: and his name shall be called Wonderful, Counseller, **The mighty God**, The everlasting Father, The Prince of Peace. *Isaiah 9:6*

And Jesus, when he was baptized, went up straightway out of the water: and, lo, the heavens were opened unto him, and he saw the Spirit of God descending like a dove, and lighting upon him: And, lo, a voice from heaven, saying, **This is my beloved Son**, in whom I am well pleased. *Matthew 3:16-17*

All things are delivered unto me of my Father: and no man knoweth the Son, but the Father; **neither knoweth any man the Father, save the Son**, and he to whomsoever the Son will reveal him. *Matthew 11:27*

And immediately Jesus stretched forth his hand, and caught him, and said unto him, O thou of little faith, wherefore didst thou doubt? And when they were come into the ship, the wind ceased. Then they that were in the ship came and worshipped him, saying, **Of a truth thou art the Son of God.** *Matthew 14:31-33*

And Simon Peter answered and said, **Thou art the Christ**, the Son of the living God. *Matthew 16:16*

Now when the centurion, and they that were with him, watching Jesus, saw the earthquake, and those things that were done, they feared greatly, saying, **Truly this was the Son of God.** *Matthew 27:54*

The beginning of the gospel of **Jesus Christ, the Son of God**. *Mark 1:1*

And the angel answered and said unto her, The Holy Ghost shall come upon thee, and the power of the Highest shall overshadow thee: therefore also **that holy thing which shall be born of thee shall be called the Son of God**. *Luke 1:35*

And **devils also came out of many, crying out**, and saying, Thou art Christ the Son of God. And he rebuking *them* suffered them not to speak: for they knew that he was Christ. *Luke 4:41*

When he saw Jesus, he cried out, and fell down before him, and with a loud voice said, What have I to do with thee, Jesus, *thou* **Son of God most high**? I beseech thee, torment me not. *Luke 8:28*

And the Word was made flesh, and dwelt among us, (and we beheld his glory, the glory as of the only begotten of the Father,) **full of grace and truth**. *John 1:14*

No man hath seen God at any time; the only begotten Son, **which is in the bosom of the Father**, he hath declared him. *John 1:18*

For God so loved the world, that he gave **his only begotten Son**, that whosoever believeth in him should not perish, but have everlasting life. For God sent not his Son into the world to condemn the world; but that the world through him might be saved. *John 3:16-17*

The Son can do nothing of himself, but what he seeth the Father do: for what things soever he doeth, these also doeth the Son likewise. For the **Father loveth the Son**, and sheweth him all things that himself doeth: and he will shew him greater works than these, that ye may marvel. For as the Father raiseth up the dead, and quickeneth them; even so the Son quickeneth whom he will. For the Father judgeth no man, but hath committed all judgment unto the Son: That **all men should honour the Son**, even as they honour the Father. He that honoureth not the Son honoureth not the Father which hath sent him. Verily, verily, I say unto you, The hour is coming, and now is, when **the dead shall hear the voice of the Son of God**: and they that hear shall live. For as the Father hath life in himself; so hath he given to the Son to have life in himself. *John 5:19-23, 25-26*

Then said Jesus unto the twelve, Will ye also go away? Then Simon Peter answered him, Lord, to whom shall we go? thou hast the words of eternal life. And **we believe and are sure that thou art that Christ. the Son of the living God.** *John 6:67-69*

When Jesus heard *that*, he said, This sickness is not unto death, but for the glory of God, **that the Son of God might be glorified** thereby. *John 11:4*

She saith unto him, Yea, Lord: **I believe that thou art the Christ, the Son of God**, which should come into the world. *John 11:27*

And whatsoever ye shall ask in my name, that will I do, **that the Father may be glorified in the Son.** *John 14:13*

These words spake Jesus, and lifted up his eyes to heaven, and said, Father, the hour is come; **glorify thy Son**, that thy Son also may glorify thee. *John 17:1*

And Thomas answered and said unto him, **My Lord and my God.** *John 20:28*

But these are written, that ye might believe that Jesus is the Christ, the Son of God; and that believing **ye might have life through his name.** *John 20:31*

The God of Abraham, and of Isaac, and of Jacob, the God of our fathers, **hath glorified his Son Jesus.** *Acts 3:13*

Concerning his Son Jesus Christ our Lord, which was made of the seed of David according to the flesh; And **declared to be the Son of God with power**, according to the spirit of holiness, by the resurrection from the dead. *Romans 1:3-4*

For what the law could not do, in that it was weak through the flesh, **God sending his own Son in the likeness of sinful flesh**, and for sin, condemned sin in the flesh. *Romans 8:3*

For whom he did foreknow, he also did predestinate **to be conformed to the image of his Son**, that he might be the firstborn among many brethren. *Romans 8:29*

For the Son of God, Jesus Christ, who was preached among you by us, *even by me and Silvanus and Timotheus, was not yea and nay, but* **in him was yea**. *II Corinthians 1:19*

But when the fulness of the time was come, God sent forth his Son, **made of a woman**, made under the law. *Galatians 4:4*

I am crucified with Christ: nevertheless I live; yet not I, but Christ liveth in me: and the life which I now live in the flesh I live by **the faith of the Son of God, who loved me, and gave himself for me**. *Galatians 2:20*

Till we all come in the unity of the faith, and of **the knowledge of the Son of God**, unto a perfect man, unto the measure of the stature of the fulness of Christ. *Ephesians 4:13*

Let this mind be in you, which was also in Christ Jesus: Who, **being in the form of God**, thought it not robbery to be equal with God. *Philippians 2:5-6*

Who hath delivered us from the power of darkness, and hath translated us into the kingdom of his dear Son: In whom we have redemption through his blood, even the forgiveness of sins: Who is **the image of the invisible God**, the firstborn of every creature: For **by him were all things created**, that are in heaven, and that are in earth, visible and invisible, whether they be thrones, or dominions, or principalities, or powers: all things were created by him, and for him: And he is before all things, and by him all things consist. And he is **the head of the body**, the church: who is the beginning, the firstborn from the dead; that in all things he might have the preeminence. For it pleased the Father that **in him should all fulness dwell**. *Colossians 1:13-19*

For in him dwelleth all the **fulness of the Godhead bodily**. *Colossians 2:9*

GOD, who at sundry times and in divers manners spake in time past unto the fathers by the prophets, Hath in these last days **spoken unto us by his Son**, whom he hath appointed **heir of all things**, **by whom also he made the worlds**; Who being the **brightness of his glory**, and the **express image of his person**, and upholding all things by the word of his power, when he had by himself purged our sins, sat down on the right hand of the Majesty on high. *Hebrews 1:1-3*

Seeing then that we have **a great high priest**, that is passed into the heavens, Jesus the Son of God, let us hold fast *our* profession. *Hebrews 4:14*

Without father, without mother, without descent, having neither beginning of days, nor end of life; but made like unto the Son of God; **abideth a priest continually**. *Hebrews 7:3*

He that committeth sin is of the devil; for the devil sinneth from the beginning. For this purpose the Son of God was manifested, **that he might destroy the works of the devil**. *I John 3:8*

In this was manifested the love of God toward us, because that God sent his only begotten Son into the world, **that we might live through him**. Herein is love, not that we loved God, but that he loved us, and sent his Son to be the propitiation for our sins. *I John 4:9-10*

Whosoever shall confess that Jesus is the Son of God, God dwelleth in him, and he in God. *I John 4:15*

Who is he that overcometh the world, but he that believeth that Jesus is the Son of God? *I John 5:5*

These things have I written unto you that believe on the name of the Son of God; that ye **may know that ye have eternal life**, and that ye may believe on the name of the Son of God. *I John 5:12*

And we know that the Son of God is come, and hath given us an understanding, that we may know him that is true, and we are in him that is true, *even* in his Son Jesus Christ. This is the **true God, and eternal life**. *I John 5:20*

And unto the angel of the church in Thyatira write; These things saith the Son of God, who hath **his eyes like unto a flame of fire, and his feet** *are* **like fine brass**. *Revelation 2:18*

I PRAISE JESUS BECAUSE HE IS...

The Son of Man

One like the Son of man came with the clouds of heaven, and came to the Ancient of days, and they brought him near before him. And there was given him dominion, and glory, and a kingdom, that all people, nations, and languages, should serve him: **his dominion is an everlasting dominion**, which shall not pass away, and his kingdom that which shall not be destroyed. *Daniel 7:13-14*

For the Son of man is **Lord even of the sabbath day**. *Matthew 12:8*

For as Jonas was three days and three nights in the whale's belly; so shall the Son of man be **three days and three nights in the heart of the earth**. *Matthew 12:40*

For **the Son of man shall come in the glory of his Father** with his angels; and then he shall reward every man according to his works. *Matthew 16:27*

And Jesus said unto them, Verily I say unto you, That ye which have followed me, in the regeneration when **the Son of man shall sit in the throne of his glory**, ye also shall sit upon twelve thrones, judging the twelve tribes of Israel. *Matthew 19:28*

Even as the Son of man came **not to be ministered unto**, but to minister, and to give his life a ransom for many. *Matthew 20:28*

For as the lightning cometh out of the east, and shineth even unto the west; so shall also the coming of the Son of man be. *Matthew 24:27*

And then shall appear the sign of the Son of man in heaven: and then shall all the tribes of the earth mourn, and they shall see the Son of man **coming in the clouds of heaven with power and great glory**. *Matthew 24:30*

When the Son of man shall come in his glory, and **all the holy angels** with him, then shall he sit upon the throne of his glory. *Matthew 25:31*

But that ye may know that the Son of man **hath power upon earth to forgive sins**, (he said unto the sick of the palsy,) I say unto thee, Arise, and take up thy couch, and go into thine house. *Luke 5:24*

The Son of man **must suffer many things**, and be rejected of the elders and chief priests and scribes, and be slain, and be raised the third day. *Luke 9:22*

For the Son of man is not come to destroy men's lives, but to **save them**. *Luke 9:56*

Also I say unto you, **Whosoever shall confess me before men**, him shall the Son of man also confess before the angels of God. *Luke 12:8*

For the Son of man is come to **seek and to save** that which was lost. *Luke 19:10*

And he saith unto him, Verily verily, I say unto you, Hereafter ye shall see heaven open, and **the angels of God ascending and descending upon the Son of man**. *John 1:51*

And no man hath ascended up to heaven, but **he that came down from heaven,** *even* the Son of man which is in heaven. *John 3:13*

And hath given him **authority to execute judgment** also, because he is the Son of man. *John 5:27*

Labour not for the meat which perisheth, but for that meat which endureth unto everlasting life, which the Son of man shall give unto you: **for him hath God the Father sealed**. *John 6:27*

Therefore, when he was gone out, Jesus said, **Now is the Son of man glorified**, and God is glorified in him. *John 13:31*

And said, Behold, I see the heavens opened, and **the Son of man standing on the right hand of God.** *Acts 7:56*

And in the midst of the seven candlesticks *one* like unto the Son of man, **clothed with a garment down to the foot, and girt about the paps with a golden girdle.** *Revelation 1:13*

I Praise Jesus Because He…

I PRAISE JESUS BECAUSE HE…

Cares, Has Compassion, Loves

But when he saw the multitudes, **he was moved with compassion** on them, because they fainted, and were scattered abroad, as sheep having no shepherd. *Matthew 9:36*

And Jesus went forth, and saw a great multitude, and was moved with compassion toward them, and **he healed their sick**. *Matthew 14:14*

Then Jesus called his disciples unto him, and said, I have compassion on the multitude, because they continue with me now three days, and have nothing to eat: and **I will not send them away fasting**, lest they faint in the way. *Matthew 15:32*

So Jesus had compassion on them, and touched their eyes: and **immediately their eyes received sight**, and they followed him. *Matthew 20:34*

And Jesus, moved with compassion, put forth *his* hand, and touched him, and saith unto him, I will; **be thou clean**. *Mark 1:41*

And when the Lord saw her**, he had compassion on her**, and said unto her, Weep not. *Luke 7:13*

Now before the feast of the passover, when Jesus knew that his hour was come that he should depart out of this world unto the Father, having loved his own which were in the world, **he loved them unto the end**. *John 13:1*

A new commandment I give unto you, That ye love one another; **as I have loved you**, that ye also love one another. *John 13:34*

As the Father hath loved me, so have I loved you: continue ye in my love. This is my commandment, That ye love one another, as I have loved you. *John 15:9, 12*

I am crucified with Christ: nevertheless I live; yet not I, but **Christ liveth in me**: and the life which I now live in the flesh I live by the faith of the

Son of God, who loved me, and gave himself for me. *Galatians 2:20*

And **walk in love**, as Christ also hath loved us, and hath given himself for us an offering and a sacrifice to God for a sweet-smelling savour. *Ephesians 5:2*

Husbands, love your wives, even as Christ also loved the church, and **gave himself** for it. *Ephesians 5:25*

I PRAISE JESUS BECAUSE HE...

Has Power & Authority

And when he had called unto *him* his twelve disciples, he gave them **power *against* unclean spirits**, to cast them out, and t**o heal all manner of sickness and all manner of disease**. *Matthew 10:1*

And then shall appear the sign of the Son of man in heaven: and then shall all the tribes of the earth mourn, and they shall see the Son of man coming in the clouds of heaven with **power and great glory**. *Matthew 24:30*

Jesus saith unto him, Thou hast said: nevertheless I say unto you, Hereafter shall ye see the Son of man sitting **on the right hand of power**, and coming in the clouds of heaven. *Matthew 26:64*

And Jesus came and spake unto them, saying, **All power** is given unto me in heaven and in earth. *Matthew 28:18*

And they were astonished at his doctrine: for his word was with power. And they were all amazed, and spake among themselves, saying, What a word is this! **for with authority and power he commandeth the unclean spirits**, and they come out. *Luke 4:32, 36*

And it came to pass on a certain day, as he was teaching, that there were Pharisees and doctors of the law sitting by, which were come out of every town of Galilee, and Judaea, and Jerusalem: and **the power of the Lord was *present* to heal them**. *Luke 5:17*

But that ye may know that the Son of man hath **power upon earth to forgive sins**, (he said unto the sick of the palsy,) I say unto thee, Arise, and take up thy couch, and go into thine house. And immediately he rose up before them, and took up that whereon he lay, and departed to his own house, glorifying God. And they were all amazed, and they glorified God, and were filled with fear, saying, We have seen strange things to day. *Luke 5:24-26*

Then he called his twelve disciples together, and gave them **power and authority** over all devils, and to cure diseases. *Luke 9:1*

And as he was yet a-coming, the devil threw him down, and tare him. And Jesus rebuked the unclean spirit, and healed the child, and delivered him again to his father. And they were **all amazed at the mighty power of God**. *Luke 9:42-43*

Hereafter shall the Son of man sit on the right hand of the power of God. *Luke 22:69*

But as many as received him, to them **gave he power to become the sons of God**, even to them that believe on his name. *John 1:12*

Therefore doth my Father love me, because I lay down my life, that I might take it again. No man taketh it from me, but I lay it down of myself. I have power to lay it down, and **I have power to take it again**. This commandment have I received of my Father. *John 10:17-18*

These words spake Jesus, and lifted up his eyes to heaven, and said, Father, the hour is come; glorify thy Son, that thy Son also may glorify thee: As thou hast given him **power over all flesh**, that he should give eternal life to as many as thou hast given him. *John 17:1-2*

How God anointed Jesus of Nazareth **with the Holy Ghost and with power**: who went about doing good, and healing all that were oppressed of the devil; for God was with him. *Acts 10:38*

And **declared *to be* the Son of God with power**, according to the spirit of holiness, by the resurrection from the dead. *Romans 1:4*

But unto them which are called, both Jews and Greeks, **Christ the power of God**, and the wisdom of God. *I Corinthians 1:24*

And he said unto me, My grace is sufficient for thee: for my strength is made perfect in weakness. Most gladly therefore will I rather glory in my infirmities, that **the power of Christ may rest upon me**. *II Corinthians 12:9*

That I may know him, and **the power of his resurrection**, and the fellowship of his sufferings, being made comformable unto his death. *Philippians 3:10*

I can do all things **through Christ** which strengtheneth me. *Philippians 4:13*

And ye are complete in him, which is the **head of all principality and power**. *Colossians 2:10*

Who being the brightness of *his* glory, and the express image of his person, and upholding all things **by the word of his power**, when he had by himself purged our sins, sat down on the right hand of the Majesty on high. *Hebrews 1:3*

For we have not followed cunningly devised fables, when we made known unto you the **power and coming** of our Lord Jesus Christ, but were eyewitnesses of his majesty. *II Peter 1:16*

Saying with a loud voice, Worthy is the Lamb that was slain to receive power, and riches, and wisdom, and strength, and honour, and glory, and blessing. And every creature which is in heaven, and on the earth, and under the earth, and such as are in the sea, and all that are in them, heard I saying, Blessing, and honour, and glory, and **power, be unto him that sitteth upon the throne, and unto the lamb for ever and ever**. *Revelation 5:12-13*

And I heard a loud voice saying in heaven, Now is come salvation, and strength, and the kingdom of our God, and **the power of his Christ**: for the accuser of our brethren is cast down, which accused them before our God day and night. *Revelation 12:10*

I PRAISE JESUS BECAUSE HE...

Heals

But he was wounded for our transgressions, he was bruised for our iniquities: the chastisement of our peace was upon him; and **with his stripes** we are healed. *Isaiah 53:5*

And Jesus went about all Galilee, teaching in their synagogues, and preaching the gospel of the kingdom, and healing **all manner of sickness** and all manner of disease among the people. And his fame went throughout all Syria: and they brought unto him all sick people that were taken with divers diseases and torments, and those which were possessed with devils, and those which were lunatick, and those that had the palsy; and he healed them. *Matthew 4:23-24*

The centurion answered and said, Lord, I am not worthy that thou shouldest come under my roof: but **speak the word only**, and my servant shall be healed. And Jesus said unto the centurion, Go thy way; and as thou hast believed, so be it done unto thee. And his servant was healed in the selfsame hour. *Matthew 8:8, 13*

When the even was come, they brought unto him many that were possessed with devils: and he cast out the spirits **with *his* word**, and healed all that were sick. *Matthew 8:16*

And Jesus went about all the cities and villages, teaching in their synagogues, and preaching the gospel of the kingdom, and **healing every sickness** and every disease among the people. *Matthew 9:35*

But when Jesus knew *it*, he withdrew himself from thence: and great multitudes followed him, and **he healed them all**. *Matthew 12:15*

Then was brought unto him one possessed with a devil, blind, and dumb: and he healed him, insomuch that **the blind and dumb both spake and saw**. *Matthew 12:22*

And Jesus went forth, and saw a great multitude, and was **moved with compassion** toward them, and he healed their sick. *Matthew 14:14*

And great multitudes came unto him, having with them those that were lame, blind, dumb, maimed, and many others, and cast them down at Jesus' feet; and he healed them: Insomuch that the multitude wondered, when they saw the dumb to speak, the maimed to be whole, the lame to walk, and the blind to see: and **they glorified the God of Israel**. *Matthew 15:30-31*

And great multitudes followed him; and he healed them there. *Matthew 19:2*

So Jesus had compassion on them, and touched their eyes: and **immediately their eyes received sight**, and they followed him. *Matthew 20:34*

And **the blind and the lame** came to him in the temple; and he healed them. But when Jesus knew it, he withdrew himself from thence: and great multitudes followed him, and he healed them all. *Matthew 21:14*

For he had healed many; insomuch that **they pressed upon him for to touch him**, as many as had plagues. *Mark 3:10*

And a certain woman, which had an issue of blood twelve years, And had suffered many things of many physicians, and had spent all that she had, and was nothing bettered, but rather grew worse, When she had heard of Jesus, came in the press behind, and touched his garment. For she said, If I may touch but his clothes, I shall be whole. And **straightway the fountain of her blood was dried up**; and she felt in her body that she was healed of that plague, *Mark 5:25-29*

And whithersoever he entered, into villages, or cities, or country, they laid the sick in the streets, and besought him that they might touch if it were but the border of his garment: and **as many as touched him were made whole**. *Mark 6:56*

The Spirit of the Lord *is* upon me, because he hath anointed me to preach the gospel to the poor; he hath sent me to **heal the brokenhearted**, to preach deliverance to the captives, and recovering of sight to the blind, to set at liberty them that are bruised. *Luke 4:18*

Now when the sun was setting, all they that had any sick with divers diseases brought them unto him; and **he laid his hands on every one of**

them, and healed them. *Luke 4:40*

But so much the more went there a fame abroad of him: and **great multitudes came** together to hear, and to be healed by him of their infirmities. *Luke 5:15*

And it came to pass on a certain day, as he was teaching, that there were Pharisees and doctors of the law sitting by, which were come out of every town of Galilee, and Judaea, and Jerusalem: and **the power of the Lord was *present* to heal them**. *Luke 5:17*

And he came down with them, and stood in the plain, and the company of his disciples, and a great multitude of people out of all Judaea and Jerusalem, and from the sea coast of Tyre and Sidon, which came to hear him, and to be healed of their diseases; And they that were vexed with unclean spirits: and they were healed, And the whole multitude sought to touch him: for **there went virtue out of him, and healed them all**. *Luke 6:17-19*

And the people, when they knew it, followed him: and he received them, and spake unto them of the kingdom of God, and **healed them that had need of healing**. *Luke 9:11*

And as he was yet a-coming, the devil threw him down, and tare him. And **Jesus rebuked the unclean spirit, and healed the child**, and delivered him again to his father. *Luke 9:42*

And, behold, there was a woman which had a spirit of infirmity eighteen years, and was bowed together, and could in no wise lift up herself. And when Jesus saw her, he called her to him, and said unto her, Woman, **thou art loosed from thine infirmity**. And he laid his hands on her: and immediately she was made straight, and glorified God. *Luke 13:11-13*

And they lifted up their voices, and said, Jesus, Master, have mercy on us. And when he saw them, he said unto them, Go shew yourselves unto the priests. And it came to pass, that, as they went, they were cleansed, And one of them, when he saw that he was healed, turned back, and with a loud voice glorified God, **And fell down on his face at his feet, giving him thanks**: and he was a Samaritan. And Jesus answering said, Were there not ten cleansed? but where are the nine? There are not found that returned to give glory to God, save this stranger. *Luke 17:13-18*

By stretching forth thine hand to heal; and that **signs and wonders may be done by the name of thy holy child Jesus**. *Acts 4:30*

How God anointed Jesus of Nazareth with the Holy Ghost and with power: who went about doing good, and **healing all that were oppressed of the** devil; for God was with him. *Acts 10:38*

Who his own self bare our sins in his own body on the tree, that we, being dead to sins, should live unto righteousness: **by whose stripes ye were healed**. *I Peter 2:24*

I PRAISE JESUS BECAUSE HE...

Suffered & Died for My Sins

Surely he hath **borne our griefs**, and **carried our sorrows**: yet we did esteem him stricken, smitten of God, and afflicted. But he was **wounded for our transgressions**, he was **bruised for our iniquities**: the chastisement of our peace was upon him; and **with his stripes we are healed.**
All we like sheep have gone astray; we have turned every one to his own way; and !lie LORD hath **laid on him the iniquity of us all**. He was **oppressed**, and he was **afflicted**, yet he opened not his mouth: he is brought as a **lamb to the slaughter**, and as a sheep before her shearers is dumb, so he openeth not his mouth.
He was taken from prison and from judgment: and who shall declare his generation? for he was cut **off out** of the land of the living: for the transgression of my people was he **stricken**. And he made his grave with the wicked, and with the rich in his death; because he had done no violence, neither was any deceit in his mouth.
Yet it pleased the LORD to **bruise** him; he hath put him to grief: when thou shalt make his soul an offering for sin, he shall see his seed, he shall prolong his days, and the pleasure of the LORD shall prosper in his hand. He shall see of the travail of his soul, and shall be satisfied: by his knowledge shall my righteous servant justify many; for he shall **bear their iniquities**. *Isaiah 53:4-11*

Then did they **spit in his face**, and **buffeted him**; and **others smote *him* with the palms of their hands**, Saying, Prophesy unto us, thou Christ, Who is he that smote thee*? Matthew 26:67-68*

Then the soldiers of the governor took Jesus into the common hall, and gathered unto him the whole band *of soldiers*. And they **stripped him**, and put on him a scarlet robe. And when they had platted **a crown of thorns**, they put *it* upon his head, and a reed in his right hand: and they bowed the knee before him, and **mocked him**, saying, Hail, King of the Jews! And they **spit upon him**, and took the reed, and **smote him on the head**. And after that they had mocked him, they took the robe off from him, and put his own raiment on him, and led him away to **crucify *him***. *Matthew 27:27-31*

And the men that held Jesus mocked him, and smote *him*. And when they had blindfolded him, they **struck him on the face**, and asked him, saying, Prophesy, who is it that smote thee? And many other things **blasphemously spake they against him**. *Luke 22:63-65*

Then Pilate therefore took Jesus, and **scourged *him***. And the soldiers platted a crown of thorns, and put *it* on his head, and they put on him a purple robe, And said, Hail, King of the Jews! and they **smote him with their hands**. Pilate therefore went forth again, and saith unto them, Behold, I bring him forth to you, that ye may know that I find no fault in him. Then came Jesus forth, wearing the crown of thorns, and the purple robe. And *Pilate* saith unto them, Behold the man! When the chief priests therefore and officers saw him, they cried out, saying, Crucify *him*, crucify *him*. *John 19:1-6*

For when we were yet without strength, in due time Christ **died for the ungodly**. *Romans 5:6*

But God commendeth his love toward us, in that, **while we were yet sinners**, Christ died for us. *Romans 5:8*

Who *is* he that condemneth? *It is* Christ that died, yea rather, that is risen again, who is even at the right hand of God, who also **maketh intercession** for us. *Romans 8:34*

For to this end Christ both died, and rose, and revived, that he might be **Lord both of the dead and living**. *Romans 14:9*

For the love of Christ constraineth us; because we thus judge, that if one died for all, then were all dead. And that **he died for all**, that they which live should not henceforth live unto themselves, but unto him which died for them, and rose again. *II Corinthians 5:14-15*

For ye know the grace of our Lord Jesus Christ, that, though he was rich, yet **for your sakes he became poor**, that ye through his poverty might be rich. *II Corinthians 8:9*

For though he was crucified through weakness, yet he liveth by the power of God. For we also are weak in him, but **we shall live with him by the power of God** toward you. *II Corinthians 13:4*

I am crucified with Christ: nevertheless I live; yet not I, but Christ liveth in me: and the life which I now live in the flesh I live by the faith of the Son of God, **who loved me, and gave himself for me**. *Galatians 2:20*

For if we believe that Jesus died and rose again, even so **them also which sleep in Jesus will God bring with him.** *1 Thessalonians 4:14*

Who died for us, that, whether we wake or sleep, we should **live together with him**. *1 Thessalonians 5:10*

I PRAISE JESUS HECAUSE HE...

Rose from the Grave

From that time forth began Jesus to show unto his disciples, how that he must go unto Jerusalem, and **suffer many things** of the elders and chief priests and scribes, and be killed, and be raised again the third day. *Matthew 16:21*

And **they shall kill him**, and the third day he shall be raised again. And they were exceeding sorry. *Matthew 17:23*

He is not here: for he is risen, as he said. Come, see the place where the Lord lay. And go quickly, and tell his disciples that he is risen from the dead; and, behold, he goeth before you into Galilee; there shall ye see him; lo, I have told you. *Matthew 28:6-7*

He is not here, but is risen: **remember how he spake unto you** when he was yet in Galilee, Saying, The Son of man must be delivered into the hands of sinful men, and be crucified, and the third day rise again. *Luke 24:6-7*

Therefore doth my Father love me, because I lay down my life, that I might take it again. No man taketh it from me, but I lay it down of myself. I have power to lay it down, and **I have power to take it again.** This commandment have I received of my Father. *John 10:17-18*

Jesus said unto her, *I am the* **resurrection, and the life**: he that believeth in me, though he were dead, yet shall he live. *John 11:25*

Yet a little while, and the world seeth me no more; but ye see me: **because I live, ye shall live also**. *John 14:19*

Whom God hath raised up, having loosed the pains of death: because **it was not possible that he should be holden of it**. *Acts 2:24*

And killed the Prince of life, whom God hath raised from the dead; **whereof we are witnesses.** *Acts 3:15*

Unto you first God, **having raised up his Son Jesus**, sent him to bless you, in turning away every one of you from his iniquities. *Acts 3:26*

Be it known unto you all, and to all the people of Israel, that by the name of Jesus Christ of Nazareth, whom ye crucified, whom God raised from the dead, *even* **by him doth this man stand here before you whole**. *Acts 4:10*

The God of our fathers raised up Jesus, whom ye slew and hanged on a tree. *Acts 5:30*

Him God raised up the third day, and **showed him openly**. *Acts 10:40*

Not to all the people, but unto **witnesses chosen before of God**, *even* to us, who did eat and drink with him after he rose from the dead. *Acts 10:41*

Because he hath appointed a day, in the which **he will judge the world in righteousness by** *that* **man whom he hath ordained**; *whereof* he hath given assurance unto all *men*, in that he hath raised him from the dead. *Acts 17:31*

Now it was not written for his sake alone, that it was imputed to him; But for us also, to whom it shall be imputed, if we believe on him that raised up Jesus our Lord from the dead; Who was delivered for our offences, and was **raised again for our justification**. *Romans 4:23-25*

Therefore we are buried with him by baptism into death: that like as Christ was raised up from the dead by the glory of the Father, even so we also should walk in newness of life. For if we have been planted together in the likeness of his death, **we shall be also in the likeness of his resurrection**: Knowing that Christ being raised from the dead dieth no more; death hath no more dominion over him. *Romans 6:4-5, 9*

But if **the Spirit of him that raised up Jesus from the dead** dwell in you, he that raised up Christ from the dead shall also quicken your mortal bodies by his Spirit that dwelleth in you. *Romans 8:11*

That if thou shalt confess with thy mouth the Lord Jesus, and shalt believe in thine heart that God hath raised him from the dead, **thou shalt be saved**. *Romans 10:9*

For to this end Christ both died, and rose, and revived, that he might be

Lord both of the dead and living. *Romans 14:9*

And God hath both raised up the Lord, and **will also raise up us by his own power.** *I Corinthians 6:14*

For I delivered unto you first of all that which I also received, how that Christ died for our sins according to the scriptures; And that he was buried, and that he rose again the third day **according to the scriptures.** *I Corinthians 15:3-4*

And that he died for all, that they which live **should not henceforth live unto themselves**, but unto him which died for them, and rose again. *II Corinthians 5:15*

Which he wrought in Christ, when he raised him from the dead, and **set *him* at his own right hand in the heavenly *places*.** *Ephesians 1:20*

And hath raised *us* up together, and **made *us* sit together in heavenly *places* in Christ** Jesus. *Ephesians 2:6*

Buried with him in baptism, wherein also ye are **risen with *him*** through the faith of the operation of God, who hath raised him from the dead. *Colossians 2:12*

And to wait for his Son from heaven, whom he raised from the dead, *even* Jesus, which **delivered us from the wrath to come**. *1 Thessalonians 1:10*

For if we believe that Jesus died and rose again, even **so them also which sleep in Jesus will God bring with him.** *1 Thessalonians 4:14*

Remember that Jesus Christ of **the seed of David** was raised from the dead according to my gospel. *II Timothy 2:8*

Blessed be the God and Father of our Lord Jesus Christ, which according to his abundant mercy hath **begotten us again unto a lively hope** by the resurrection of Jesus Christ from the dead. *I Peter 1:3*

Who by him do believe in God, that raised him up from the dead, and **gave him glory**; that your faith and hope might be in God. *II Peter 1:21*

I PRAISE JESUS BECAUSE HE…

Shall Return

And then shall appear the sign of the Son of man in heaven: and then shall all the tribes of the earth mourn, and they shall see the Son of man coming in the clouds of heaven **with power and great glory.** *Matthew 24:30*

Be ye therefore ready also: for the Son of man cometh at **an hour when ye think not.** *Luke 12:40*

I tell you that he will avenge them speedily. Nevertheless when the Son of man cometh, **shall he find faith on the earth**? *Luke 18:8*

For as the lightning cometh out of the east, and shineth even unto the west; so shall also the coming of the Son of man be. *Matthew 24:27*

And then shall appear the sign of the Son of man in heaven: and then shall all the tribes of the earth mourn, and they shall see the Son of man **coming in the clouds of heaven** with power and great glory. *Matthew 24:30*

But **as the days of Noe** *were*, so shall also the coming of the Son of man be. *Matthew 24:37*

And **knew not until the flood came**, and took them all away; so shall also the coming of the Son of man be. *Matthew 24:39*

Verily, verily, I say unto you, The hour is coming, and now is, when **the dead shall hear the voice of the Son of God**: and they that hear shall live. *John 5:25*

Marvel not at this: for **the hour is coming**, in the which all that are in the graves shall hear his voice. *John 5:28*

Behold, I show you a mystery; We shall not all sleep, but we shall all be changed, In a moment, **in the twinkling of an eye**, at the last trump: for the trumpet shall sound, and the dead shall be raised incorruptible, and **we shall be changed.** For this corruptible must put on incorruption, and this mortal *must* put on immortality. So when this corruptible shall have put on incorruption, and this mortal shall have put on **immortality**, then shall be brought to pass the saying that is written, **Death is swallowed up in victory**. O death, where *is* thy sting? O grave, where *is* thy victory? The sting of death *is* sin; and the strength of sin *is* the law. But thanks *be* to God, which giveth us the victory through our Lord Jesus Christ. *I Corinthians 15:51-57*

For what *is* **our hope, or joy, or crown of rejoicing**? *Are* not even ye in the presence of our Lord Jesus Christ at his coming? *I Thessalonians 2:19*

To the end he may stablish your hearts **unblameable in holiness** before God, even our Father, at the coming of our Lord Jesus Christ with all his saints. *I Thessalonians 3:13*

But I would not have you to be ignorant, brethren, concerning them which are asleep, that ye sorrow not, even as others which have no hope. For if we believe that Jesus died and rose again, even so them also which sleep in Jesus will God bring with him. For this we say unto you by the word of the Lord, that we which are alive *and* remain unto the coming of the Lord shall not prevent them which are asleep. For the Lord himself shall descend from heaven with a shout, with the voice of the archangel, and with the trump of God: and **the dead in Christ shall rise first**: Then we which are alive *and* remain shall be **caught up together with them in the clouds**, to **meet the Lord in the air**: and **so shall we ever be with the Lord**. Wherefore comfort one another with these words.
I Thessalonians 4:13-18

And the very God of peace **sanctify you wholly**; and *I pray God* your whole spirit and soul and body be preserved **blameless** unto the coming of our Lord Jesus Christ. *I Thessalonians 5:23*

Now we beseech you, brethren, by the coming of our Lord Jesus Christ, and *by* our **gathering together unto him**. *II Thessalonians 2:1*

And then shall that **Wicked be revealed**, whom the Lord shall consume with the spirit of his mouth, and shall **destroy with the brightness of his coming**. *II Thessalonians 2:8*

Be patient therefore, brethren, unto the coming of the Lord. Behold, the husbandman waiteth for the precious fruit of the earth, and hath long patience for it, until he receive the early and latter rain. Be ye also patient; stablish your hearts: for the coming of the Lord **draweth nigh**. *James 5:7-8*

For we have not followed cunningly devised fables, when we made known unto you the power and coming of our Lord Jesus Christ, but were **eyewitnesses of his majesty**. *II Peter 1:16*

Looking for and hasting unto the coming of the day of God, wherein the heavens being on fire shall be dissolved, and the **elements shall melt with fervent heat**? *II Peter 3:12*

And now, little children, **abide in him**; that, when he shall appear, we may have confidence, and not be ashamed before him at his coming. *I John 2:28*

Personal Notes

Personal Notes

REASONS I AM THANKFUL TO GOD

REASONS I PRAISE GOD

ADDITIONAL SCRIPTURES MEANINGFUL TO ME

Personal Notes

REASONS I AM THANKFUL TO GOD

REASONS I PRAISE GOD

ADDITIONAL SCRIPTURES MEANINGFUL TO ME

Personal Notes

REASONS I AM THANKFUL TO GOD

REASONS I PRAISE GOD

ADDITIONAL SCRIPTURES MEANINGFUL TO ME

Personal Notes

REASONS I AM THANKFUL TO GOD

REASONS I PRAISE GOD

ADDITIONAL SCRIPTURES MEANINGFUL TO ME

Personal Notes

REASONS I AM THANKFUL TO GOD

REASONS I PRAISE GOD

ADDITIONAL SCRIPTURES MEANINGFUL TO ME

Personal Notes

REASONS I AM THANKFUL TO GOD

REASONS I PRAISE GOD

ADDITIONAL SCRIPTURES MEANINGFUL TO ME

Personal Notes

REASONS I AM THANKFUL TO GOD

REASONS I PRAISE GOD

ADDITIONAL SCRIPTURES MEANINGFUL TO ME

Personal Notes

REASONS I AM THANKFUL TO GOD

_____
_____
_____
_____
_____
_____
_____
_____
_____
_____

REASONS I PRAISE GOD

_____
_____
_____
_____
_____
_____
_____
_____
_____
_____

ADDITIONAL SCRIPTURES MEANINGFUL TO ME

_____
_____
_____
_____
_____
_____
_____
_____
_____

Personal Notes

REASONS I AM THANKFUL TO GOD

REASONS I PRAISE GOD

ADDITIONAL SCRIPTURES MEANINGFUL TO ME

Personal Notes

REASONS I AM THANKFUL TO GOD

_____
_____
_____
_____
_____
_____
_____
_____
_____
_____
_____

REASONS I PRAISE GOD

_____
_____
_____
_____
_____
_____
_____
_____
_____
_____
_____

ADDITIONAL SCRIPTURES MEANINGFUL TO ME

_____
_____
_____
_____
_____
_____
_____
_____
_____

Made in the USA
San Bernardino, CA
09 June 2015